DRACULA
BEYOND STOKER

Issue 5

DBS Press

Dracula Beyond Stoker
Issue 5

Tucker Christine
editor

Edward G. Pettit
Shannon Vare Christine
consulting editors

Published by DBS Press
ISBN - 978-1-963391-06-0 (Paperback)
ISBN - 978-1-963391-07-7 (e-book)
November, 2024

www.dbspress.com
www.draculabeyondstoker.com

Contents

Letter, Editor to the Reader

My dear reader,—

We share many a yarn in these pages: tales of heartache and heartbreak, accounts of daring action and thrilling adventure, encounters with devils and demons. At the heart of these stories are three very different men—Jack Seward, Quincey Morris, and Arthur Holmwood—bound by friendship, honor, and their shared love for Lucy Westenra. We've gathered an impressive array of old and new friends to explore where these men came from and where their paths might lead after the events of *Dracula*.

Mark Oxbrow takes us on an adventure with Arthur and Jack shortly after Quincey's death, while Dracula and Renfield get a visit from an incognito nobleman in Henry Herz's latest *DNR Investigative Services* installment. Elizabeth Twist and Jasmine De La Paz each delve into Seward's romantic entanglements following Lucy's tragic end. Kay Hanifen returns to tell us "How Quincey P. Morris Lost His Finest Horse and Found His Way to London," and S.L. Edwards places our ill-fated Texan in the eerie afterlife, navigating a labyrinth with another gothic martyr. The wonderful Doris V. Sutherland, always thinking outside the box, gives us a tale for each man—well each man's bloodline/legacy anyway.

Once again we've enlisted Chris McAuley to provide profiles and appreciations of these three heroes.

So settle in and turn the page, your suitors await.

Yours, as ever and always,

TUCKER

Arthur Holmwood
The Noble Heart
By Chris McAuley

Arthur Holmwood, often overshadowed by the more dramatic figures in Bram Stoker's *Dracula*, embodies the virtues of nobility, duty, and quiet strength. As the future Lord Godalming, Arthur represents the quintessential English gentleman, balancing the responsibilities of his title with the emotional turmoil that comes with his involvement in the battle against Dracula. This essay examines his role in the narrative, his symbolic significance, and his portrayal in various adaptations of *Dracula*.

Arthur is introduced to readers as a man of noble birth, soon to inherit the title of Lord Godalming. Stoker describes him as "a tall, handsome, fair-haired young man, with a firm mouth and a full jaw." He is the epitome of English aristocracy—refined, composed, honorable, and with a deep sense of duty and dignity. Arthur's engagement to Lucy Westenra further cements his role as the embodiment of Victorian ideals, as he appears to be the perfect match for the beautiful and virtuous Lucy.

His character is rooted in the traditions of English nobility. He embodies the virtues expected of an English gentleman of his time—honor, responsibility, and a strong moral compass. Unlike the more adventurous Quincey Morris or the intellectual Dr. Seward, Arthur's strength lies in his steadfastness and reliability. He is not a man of grand gestures or daring deeds, but rather one of quiet determination and unwavering support for those he loves. This makes him a pillar of strength in the face of the horrors that unfold around him.

His love for Lucy is genuine and deep, and his grief over her illness and subsequent death is palpable. Arthur's reaction to Lucy's transformation into a vampire is one of the most heart-breaking moments in the novel. It is Arthur who, with trembling hands, drives the stake through her heart, releasing her from the curse of the undead. This act, though painful, highlights Arthur's strength of character and his commitment to doing what is right, no matter the personal cost.

Arthur's role as Lucy's fiancé also serves to underscore his emotional journey. His sorrow is not just for Lucy's death but for the loss of a life that will never be. This humanizes Arthur making him more than just a symbol of nobility, but a man deeply affected by the events around him.

Within the group of vampire hunters, Arthur's role is often that of the moral center. His title and social standing give him a certain authority, but it is his decency and sense of duty that truly earn him the respect of his peers. Arthur may not be the strategist like Van Helsing or the man of action like Quincey, but his presence is crucial to the group's cohesion. He brings a sense of purpose and legitimacy to their mission, representing the fight against evil as a noble cause.

Arthur's wealth and status also play a practical role in the group's efforts. As Lord Godalming, he has access to resources that aid their quest, from securing transport to providing a safe haven. However, Arthur's contributions are not limited to material support. His emotional resilience and ability to maintain hope in the darkest of times provide the group with the strength they need to continue their fight against Dracula.

Arthur serves as a symbol of the British aristocracy during a time of great social and cultural change. His character represents the virtues that were expected of the English upper class. However, Stoker uses Arthur to explore the limitations of these ideals in the face of true horror. While Arthur's nobility and sense of duty are admirable, they are not enough to shield him from the devastating effects of Dracula's influence. His journey from a confident, soon-to-be lord to a man deeply scarred by loss and grief reflects the broader anxieties of the Victorian era. As the old social order began to crumble, characters like Arthur symbolized both the strengths and weaknesses of a class that was struggling to maintain its relevance in a changing world. In this sense, Arthur's character is not just a representation of the aristocracy, but a commentary on its fragility in the face of new, unsettling forces.

Arthur Holmwood and Count Dracula are stark contrasts, both in their backgrounds and their values. Arthur, with his English heritage and noble blood, represents the civilized, orderly world that Dracula seeks to undermine. Dracula, with his ancient, corrupted lineage, is the antithesis of everything Arthur stands for—chaos, darkness, and moral decay. This opposition between Arthur and Dracula is not just a personal conflict but a symbolic battle between good and evil, light and darkness.

Arthur's role as a foil to Dracula is particularly evident in the way he reacts to the vampire's threat. While Dracula operates in the shadows, corrupting and destroying lives, Arthur's actions are driven by a desire to protect and preserve. His decision to end Lucy's vampiric existence, painful as it is, reflects his commitment to restoring order and morality. In this sense, Arthur's struggle against Dracula is not just a physical battle but a moral one, representing the fight to uphold the values of civilization against the encroaching darkness.

While Arthur Holmwood is a character of significant importance, his portrayal in *Dracula* has been critiqued for its lack of depth compared to other characters. Some readers may find Arthur too reserved or even bland, especially when contrasted with more dynamic figures like Quincey Morris or Van Helsing. His noble demeanor, while admirable, can sometimes come across as distant or aloof, making it harder for readers to connect with him on an emotional level.

Moreover, Arthur's character development is somewhat limited by the novel's focus on other characters. While his grief and bravery are explored, his inner thoughts and struggles are not as fully realized as those of characters like Jonathan Harker or Mina. This can leave Arthur feeling more like a symbol than a fully fleshed-out character, a figure who serves the plot but does not transcend it.

Film and media portrayals of Holmwood have varied widely, reflecting different interpretations of his character. In some, Arthur is depicted as a strong, decisive figure, embodying the virtues of the English aristocracy. In others, his role is downplayed or altered, with his character sometimes merged with others, such as Jonathan Harker or Quincey Morris, to streamline the narrative.

In Francis Ford Coppola's *Bram Stoker's Dracula* (1992), Arthur, played by Cary Elwes, is portrayed as a handsome, brave, and somewhat tortured figure, deeply in love with Lucy and devastated by her death. This adaptation gives Arthur more emotional depth and screen time, highlighting his internal struggle and his role in the fight against Dracula.

Other adaptations have taken liberties with Arthur's character, reimagining him in different contexts or emphasizing different aspects of his personality. These portrayals reflect the flexibility of Arthur's character, allowing him to be adapted to suit various narrative needs while still retaining the core elements of his noble and honorable nature.

Despite any critiques, Arthur Holmwood's legacy in *Dracula* remains significant. He represents a key aspect of the novel's exploration of Victorian society, embodying the values and responsibilities of the English aristocracy. His journey through love, loss, and moral conflict adds depth to the novel's exploration of good versus evil.

Arthur's role in *Dracula* also highlights the novel's themes of sacrifice and duty. His willingness to do what is necessary, even when it means confronting his worst fears, speaks to the courage required to face the unknown. In this way, Arthur's character continues to resonate with readers and audiences, serving as a reminder that true nobility lies not in birthright, but in the strength to do what is right, no matter the cost.

Arthur's significance lies not in grand gestures or dramatic heroics, but in his unwavering commitment to duty and the people he loves. He represents the best of the old world, a figure of stability and moral clarity in a narrative that often teeters on the edge of darkness. Through Arthur Holmwood, Stoker offers readers a glimpse of the noble heart that beats within the *Dracula* saga, a heart that continues to inspire and captivate more than a century after the novel's publication.

Dime Novels, Penny Dreadfuls
By Mark Oxbrow

'Whatever unhappy wretch reads these lines may bid adieu to the world and all hope, for they are doomed! 'They will never emerge from these vaults with life, for there is a hideous secret…so awful and so hideous, that to write it makes one's blood curdle, and the flesh to creep upon my bones.'

—*Sweeney Todd, the Demon Barber of Fleet Street*—OR— *The String of Pearls.*, Penny Dreadful, London 1846-1847

Journal of Arthur Holmwood, Lord Godalming

9 November 1893

Quincey is dead.

Three nights ago, at Castle Dracula, I failed him, as I failed Lucy. As I fail all those that I love.

There was a girl among the Romany.

Thirteen perhaps? No more than fourteen years. Her coal-black hair braided and tied with ribbon. She huddled close to the leader of Dracula's thralls.

Their leiter-wagon bore Dracula, buried in a box of earth.

We wove the final miles around the mountainside. Wolves at our heels. The girl whipping at the horses as the cart burst across the bridge into the courtyard.

The Romany drew daggers and butchers' knives, fired on us with revolvers. Fearsome, deadly men: bearded, mustached, wearing furs and leather.

Harker threw himself into the fray. Quincey hacked a path toward the cart with his Bowie knife.

The girl weaved through the battle. Half in shadow. She smiled at me, and I saw the boning knife in her fist. Jack screamed my name, but I faltered. I faltered and did nothing.

The Romany girl swirled and stabbed the blade deep into Quincey's side. She clawed at his face, shrieking and ripping the knife up through his guts.

I saw Jack aim his Winchester and fire. His shot tore the girl's throat out. She swayed and staggered back. A second shot hit her temple, shattering her skull.

Jack grabbed tight hold of my shoulder, shook me, screaming in my face to fight, pushing me forward. I stumbled, raising my rifle.

I barely heard the shots. My feet dragged in the snow as I fired on the Romany and their wolves.

The box splintered under Harker and Quincey's assault, and there was Dracula, lit by the rays of the dying sun.

Dr. Seward's Diary

9 November

The villagers of Dimitrescu care for us and tend our wounds. They took us into their homes like long lost kin, fed us, warming us by their hearths. What little they have in this world they give to us freely, without a second thought.

They saw us riding the mountain path, desperate to beat the Romany back to Dracula's castle. They heard the wolves howl and the baying of their dogs, and they shuttered their windows and barred their doors.

None return from Castle Dracula.

They thought us lost, food for wolves and vampires, but we survived. We were met near the crossroads by the village priest, a timid man named Valeriu. He rang the bells, and the villagers cautiously stepped out of their homes, in the dead of night, as he laughed and cried aloud.

Aged widows and small children took our hands in theirs and blessed us. Burly men, field workers with ragged beards and tearstained faces, bade us tell the story over and again.

Dracula exultant, eyes shining red, in the shattered box.

Harker's curved Kukri knife, sharp as a razor, cutting Dracula's throat, down to the bone. Quincey Morris spitting blood and stabbing his Bowie knife deep into Dracula's heart.

The priest translated, as bottles of blueberry brandy and dark wine appeared, and the villagers lit bonfires in the streets.

Violins, tilincă pipes, and lutes named cobza, were brought out. I never heard such joyful songs. The villagers danced in the snow, in rings about the fires.

A mother handed her baby to Mrs. Harker and to Van Helsing. The infant wore a nightgown and was swaddled in lace. Perhaps she believed our touch would protect or bless her child?

Something, the mother's eyes perhaps or a braid in her hair, made me think of the Romany girl. God forgive me.

The priest had Quincey's body taken down from the cart. We had wrapped him as best we could in cloaks and overcoats. A place was made by the altar in the tiny village church. Candles were lit, and the priest had women wash the blood from the body. A crooked-back seamstress stitched up Quincey's wounds. Dozens of tiny, neat stitches.

Arthur keeps a vigil over Quincey's body each night. He will barely eat, and what sleep he permits himself is tormented and feverish.

I never thought to see him this way. To lose our dearest friend, poor beloved Lucy, and his father within so short a time. It is unbearable.

Journal of Arthur Holmwood, Lord Godalming

9 November

I hear Van Helsing drinking and dancing with the peasants. How? When Quincey lies dead.

Does he care so little?

Dr. Seward's Diary

9 November

Van Helsing took me aside as the night wore on, handing me a cigar.

Jonathan and Mrs. Harker retired for the evening. The priest gave up his lodgings. I do not know how they hoped to sleep. The village revels showed no sign of abating.

Van Helsing rattled a box of matches and lit our cigars. He seemed in good spirits. He asked me about Quincey. Wanted to know how Art and I had made his acquaintance.

An English aristocrat, a London doctor, and a two-gunned Texan.

Initially I resented his questioning, but gradually I understood the purpose behind his words.

Van Helsing would not let me dwell alone in my grief.

He nudged me, cajoling tales of happier days until, despite myself, I was smiling at the thought of my friends and our foolhardy adventures.

Dear God, has it been eight years? I had turned twenty-one on the Tuesday, and my skull was splitting, the worse for burnt rum punch and Scotch whisky. Arthur insisted I meet him promptly on Wednesday morning, 11 am, by the Albert Memorial, near Kensington Gardens.

He was being his usual mysterious self.

The Albert Memorial was a curious meeting place. Prince Albert of Saxe-Coburg-Gotha, Queen Victoria's beloved consort, died in 1861, before Art and I were born, but his ghost still haunted England.

Arthur detested anything morbid or macabre. He yearned to escape, and to see a world that appeared so bright, bursting with colour, but out of reach.

London seemed forever shrouded in black.

The Queen's mourning was without end. She refused to abandon her widow's dresses and black gloves, her veils and black Whitby jet necklaces.

'We are leaving.' Arthur announced. 'You and I are of age, and I will be damned if we'll stay another month in this Godforsaken city!'

Arthur led me widdershins around the Albert Memorial, pointing out the four cardinal groups of marble sculptures.

'Europe, Asia, Africa, or the Americas?' Arthur beamed. 'You decide! Where do we sail?'

I thought him quite mad, but I looked up the lumbering bull of Europe, at Asia and its carved elephant and tea caddy, Africa with a camel and the head of an Egyptian sphinx, and the American buffalo with a lady, like some mythic goddess, wearing a feathered headdress.

'America' I said softly.

Within the week we set sail for New York City.

Van Helsing wanted to hear every detail, no matter how slight. I told him how easily Arthur took to New York high society. He stood out in the gilded ballrooms of the Asters and the Vanderbilts: a genuine English nobleman. Quite the novelty.

Arthur Holmwood, eldest son of Lord Godalming, heir to estates in England and an ancestral castle in the Highlands of Scotland.

Arthur had the uncanny knack of finding trouble wherever we went. Not content to hobnob in polite society, Art took me to the dreaded slums of the Five Points. I think Art hoped to meet Hell-Cat Maggie or the Bowery Boys!

That summer we travelled to Massachusetts, Philadelphia and Washington D.C., where I visited the Government Hospital for the Insane. I was able to talk with doctors who treat the soldiers of the Civil War. They spoke of the 'irritable heart' that plagues so many veterans.

A nurse, an angel of comfort who tended the injured at the Battle of Gettysburg, told me of the melancholia that causes soldiers to take their own lives. Those not broken in body, may be broken in mind.

We met Quincey in California.

Arthur wanted to ride the railroads to the Pacific. Naturally, we gravitated to possibly the worst bar in San Francisco. Gambling dens, bawdy houses, saloons. This was the Barbary Coast, named for far shores plundered by notorious pirates and slavers.

'Excuse me, gentlemen. I wonder, may I take a seat?' Quincey grinned, tipping his Stetson hat when we agreed. 'Thank you kindly. Will you allow me to buy you both a drink?'

He motioned to the bartender who brought a bottle of Kentucky bourbon.

What neither Art nor I knew was that Quincey feared for our lives. He overheard a rough gang of Irishmen and Australians take exception to two English gentlemen in their saloon.

Quincey told tall tales as we drank the bottle.

He said he was raised wrangling longhorn cattle back in Texas, but rode to the California goldfields in search of adventure. He conjured stories of Paul Bunyan, the giant lumberjack, and the mighty John Henry, Billy the Kid, and the Hole-in-the-Wall Gang.

There was no more than an inch or two of bourbon left in the bottle when a drunken oaf stumbled into our table. He cursed us loudly, slurring his words and throwing a punch. I dodged the fist, but his compatriot, an Australian ticket of leave man, drew a revolver and pulled the trigger.

The bullet struck Arthur. He reeled back, but before he hit the floor, Quincey was standing tall, Bowie knife in hand. He fought the Australian for the gun and slashed the Bowie knife across the man's face, slicing through his nose and left eye.

Quincey shoved the man to the saloon floor, grinding his face in blood and sawdust and splintered glass.

The bullet was lodged deep in Arthur's shoulder, perilously close to the brachial artery. I do not pretend to be a surgeon, but I was glad of my anatomy classes as I dug the bullet out.

Quincey paid a lady to fetch a particular dressmaker from Chinatown. She sewed up Arthur's shoulder with care, like she was hemming a skirt. It was finer needlework than I ever saw from a London physician.

That bloody night bound us together, and we became inseparable.

Journal of Arthur Holmwood, Lord Godalming

11 November

We said our farewells to Dimitrescu and its rustic hospitality. The villagers have done all they can to raise my spirits, but I fear it is impossible. I am lost.

The village cabinetmaker, a Mr. Roşu, has built a coffin for Quincey's body. He tells me it is built of oak and rosewood. I never saw its equal.

Jack reminded me, as we gathered up our belongings, of the night we met Quincey, and the battle of the Barbary Coast.

He recalled the ancient Chinese woman that stitched me back together, as if she was repairing a tear in a shirt sleeve.

The wound healed years ago, barely leaving a scar, but my shoulder still troubles me on winter nights.

Dr. Seward's Diary

12 November

We met the Orient Express at Budapest. Our journey takes us through Vienna, Strasbourg, and Munich to Paris Gare de l'Est.

Arthur sits in the baggage carriage, watching over Quincey's coffin. Harker and Mina have a private compartment. I sit, smoking cigars and drinking Napoleon brandy, with the professor.

Van Helsing asked me how Arthur is fairing. I did not know what to tell him. I fear for my friend.

The professor enquired about Quincey's kin.

Quincey confided that his mother and father both died of yellow fever. He lost a sister in childbirth, and another disappeared in New Orleans during the Civil War.

I could not rightly tell Van Helsing how Quincey came by his fortune.

Quincey made a game of the story, telling anyone that asked a different tale. His grandmother invested in the Buffalo Bayou, Brazos, and Colorado Railway. His father was the bounty hunter that shot the outlaw Hoodoo Brown in Dodge City. Quincey won a treasure map in a poker game, beat a woman named 'Diamondback' and found a buried crate of Confederate gold. Aces and eights.

I don't believe that we ever heard the truth of it.

Arthur, Quincey, and I took stagecoaches from California, across Nevada, the Territories of Idaho and Wyoming, Nebraska and Iowa. We crossed the Great Plains and the Rocky Mountains.

The Orient Express is a good deal more comfortable than the Deadwood Stage.

Quincey wiled away the hours with his nose buried in Dime Novels. He regaled us with exotic tales of gunslingers, bandits, and train robbers.

On Hallowe'en night, we huddled around a campfire in the prairies, cooked bacon and beans, and told ghost stories.

Quincey shared a tale of the Guajona that he heard as a boy. The Guajona is a loathsome hag, the wicked witch of New Mexico. This vile creature uses a curious snaggletooth to drink the blood of children.

I felt it was a matter of honour to defend the English ghost story. I recalled a visit I made to Wharram Percy in the Wolds of North Yorkshire. The village thrived in medieval times, but it was utterly abandoned, left to ruin.

An Oxford acquaintance spent a summer conducting an archeological dig there and found dreadful things.

Hundreds of human skulls and bones. Not buried with dignity but hacked apart, dismembered, and burned. Men, women, children.

Violently decapitated with cut marks on their skulls. Did our starving English ancestors turn to cannibalism in times of famine? Did they eat the flesh of the dead? Or did they fear something worse: that these corpses would rise from their graves as Revenants, the Un-Dead? We may never know. The village buried its secrets deep.

Arthur, not to be outdone, put aside his distaste for the Gothic. He told a tale from his childhood in the Highlands of Scotland. Art's mother is Lady Blacklunans, born and raised in Glenshee, halfway between Glamis Castle and Queen Victoria's estate at Balmoral.

Glamis Castle keeps a dreadful secret.

It is whispered that there is a curse upon Glamis and the Bowes-Lyon family. A grotesque thing is kept hidden away in the depths of the castle. The Monster of Glamis lives out its days and nights imprisoned, tended by servants.

The secret is revealed to the sons of the Bowes-Lyon family when they come of age. Anyone that attempts to unravel the mystery is warned it will unhinge their mind.

I persuaded Arthur to join us in the restaurant carriage for dinner. My efforts were rewarded with the faintest of smiles as Art recalled a rather less splendid dinner on the shores of Lake Titicaca.

Van Helsing gently coaxed Arthur to share stories of our travels. Riding across Bolivia and Peru. Trading with the Mapuches, watching them hunt with bolas and deadly long spears. We journeyed west from the Pampas, sailing from Chile to the Marquesas Islands with a plan to make fortunes trading sandalwood to China!

The sandalwood trade was lucrative, but it attracted unscrupulous men: escaped convicts, brigands and pirates. We were fortunate to escape the Marquesas with nothing worse than cuts and bruises.

There is a thin line between fearless and foolhardy.

Journal of Arthur Holmwood, Lord Godalming

12 November

I have misjudged Van Helsing.

He spoke kindly of Quincey this evening. Recalled his stout heart and fierce loyalty.

Van Helsing told me that Quincey did not sleep but guarded Lucy, dusk till dawn. He paced the gardens, carrying his Winchester in the crook of his arm.

Gods. Jack and I took shifts to sleep and to keep a watch, but Quincey never faltered for a moment.

Van Helsing ordered a bottle of single-malt Scotch whisky and filled our glasses. Jack and I spoke of Argentina and the Marquesas, sailing the Korean Strait, and nearly losing our heads to a samurai in Japan.

We raised a glass and toasted absent friends.

Dr. Seward's Diary

19 November

It was raining as we arrived in London.

Everything was so familiar and yet the city seems strange to me. I found myself staring into the puddles. Watching raindrops splash in the muddy water.

I must not forget to collect more vials of chloral hydrate.

Ladies and gentlemen bustle down Piccadilly, heels clicking, going hither and thither. Carrying hat boxes and taking afternoon tea. Trams rattle along Oxford Street. Children sail toy boats on the pond at Kensington Gardens.

Nothing has changed, but it will never be the same.

It was a blessing to sleep a night in my own bed.

We met for luncheon at Verrey's Cafe Restaurant in Regent Street. It was one of Quincey's beloved haunts.

There was a parting of the ways soon after Tokyo. My mother was taken ill, and Arthur accompanied me back to England.

Fate brought Quincey to London in May 1887. He had fallen in with William Cody in South Dakota and joined Buffalo Bill's Wild West show. Quincey was a rough rider, playing a 7th Cavalry man at the Custer massacre at Little Bighorn.

Henry Irving and Mr. Stoker of the Lyceum Theatre met Mr. Cody as they toured America. A year later he arrived in London with a hundred Sioux, Cheyenne, Kiowa, Pawnee and Ogala, cowboys, Mexican wild riders, a herd of buffaloes, bronchos, Texas steers, elk, bears, and our dearest friend, Mr. Quincey P. Morris.

Quincey formally introduced Arthur, Lucy, and I to Buffalo Bill Cody at Oatlands Park that June. It was a fine afternoon. Irving and Stoker rode in a carriage with Cody, to the cheers of an enthusiastic London crowd. Lucy and Mina rode with Florence Stoker, Miss. Ellen Terry, and the legendary sharpshooters, Miss. Annie Oakley and Miss. Lillian Smith, the California Huntress.

After six months performing at Earl's Court, Quincey decided to leave the Wild West show and make a home for himself in London. William Cody gifted him a piebald horse, and Quincey found a quaint apartment near Grosvenor Square, in Mayfair.

I have often wondered what the passersby thought when they saw a Texan cowboy gallop his horse across Hyde Park in the springtime!

London will be quieter and lonelier without Quincey.

As we took tea at Verrey's, Arthur raised the delicate subject of the burial. Quincey had no family mausoleum in Texas. London has the Necropolis Railway, and the seven great cemeteries, but it is hard to imagine Quincey entombed in a City of the Dead.

Mina wondered if Quincey may not be buried near to Lucy. We said little, but soundly dissuaded her of the notion.

It was Harker that suggested Arthur's ancestral home in Scotland. Quincey loved the Highlands. Of all the places that he stayed in Britain, Quincey was happiest and most free at Castle Blacklunans.

Journal of Arthur Holmwood, Lord Godalming

20 November

Castle Blacklunans. I sent a telegram to my mother. I doubt she expected so grim a party to descend upon her.

She has hidden herself away in the castle since father's death. Ordinarily she would have returned to England, staying until spring, but she seems determined to see out the winter months in Scotland.

Kings Cross, York, Berwick-upon-Tweed, Edinburgh, over the Forth Rail Bridge to Fife, Cupar, across the Tay Bridge to Dundee. The train was quiet. We were delayed near Peterborough when a tree branch fell upon the tracks.

The porters at Edinburgh doffed their hats and offered condolences for my loss.

We will take a coach and horses from Dundee to the castle. So like the Romany and their wolves, but this time it is not Dracula nailed into the box, carried on a cart.

Dr. Seward's Diary

22 November

May till October, Walpurgisnacht to Hallowe'en, Quincey rode with Buffalo Bill's rough riders of the world.

In October 1887 he took his leave, and Arthur invited Quincey to Scotland, deer stalking at Castle Blacklunans.

Mina insisted that Quincey must have a fine suit of clothes from a Highland outfitter. Quincey had shirts, a waistcoat and Harris tweed jacket tailor made, and a pair of stout leather boots. Arthur had him fitted for a kilt, in Robertson hunting tartan, despite Quincey's protestations that his knees were not fit to be seen in polite society!

Arthur took Quincey to Alexander Henry of Edinburgh to find a stalking rifle. It is not appropriate to shoot stags in the Highlands with a Winchester Model 1886 lever-action repeating rifle. Quincey chose a fine single barrel breech-loading rifle with a 28-inch barrel and polished walnut stock.

Quincey immediately fell in love with the Highlands. Blacklunans lies about twenty-two miles north-west of Glamis Castle, in the heart of Glenshee, in Scots Gaelic: Gleann Shith, 'the Glen of the Fairies.'

The castle itself is not as grand as Glamis or Balmoral. It was a fortified medieval tower, slighted by Sir James Douglas during the wars against King Edward the First. Arthur's great grandfather had the ruins of Blacklunans restored as a baronial castle with a hunting lodge, stables and chapel.

Arthur's mother, Euphemia, Lady Blacklunans, is as mischievous as she is eccentric. She is seldom without her long-stemmed pipe made of wood and ivory. Her clothes are purple tweed, like the mountain heather, and she is never without her sgian-dubh, a short and sharp Scots knife.

Lady Blacklunans is a close friend and confidant of Queen Victoria. She joined the Queen and John Brown, Her Majesty's Highland ghillie, as they rode ponies out across the hills. I am told that Lady Blacklunans joined séances at Balmoral, as the grieving Queen spoke with the spirit of Albert, her dead husband.

Quincey was overjoyed when we were invited to Balmoral to attend the Queen's Hallowe'en celebrations.

Buffalo Bill's Wild West gave a special performance in London. 'By command of Her Majesty, the Queen.' Cody, the Sioux Chief Red Shirt, and two squaws with papooses were presented to the Royal party.

Her Majesty was delighted to hear that one of Buffalo Bill's rough riders was a guest of Lady Blacklunans.

The Hallowe'en revels at Balmoral Castle were outlandish. Bagpipers and drums, fiery torches in procession, Queen Victoria riding in a black carriage. The Queen's youngest daughter, Princess Beatrice, seemed quite taken with Quincey.

There was hot wine, spiced with cinnamon, nutmeg, cloves, and ginger root. Wild pig roasted on a spit. A giant pyre was lit, illuminating the castle, and the effigy of a witch was thrown into the flames.

I will never forget that Hallowe'en night, or telling ghost stories by a prairie campfire.

Journal of Arthur Holmwood, Lord Godalming

22 November

My mother greeted my friends in her own peculiar way.

Jack and Harker were offered a seat by the hearth and a glass of whisky. Mrs. Harker was embraced like a lost daughter with two kisses on her face, la bise, as if we were in Paris or Florence.

Van Helsing she ignored for a time, quite rudely. Then, out of nowhere, she invited him to tour the library.

She has the strangest feelings about people sometimes. Intuition, some call it. A sixth sense. My mother calls it dà-shealladah, the second sight. She walks the worlds of the living and the dead.

Quincey's coffin was brought into the hunting hall. My mother had his body shrouded in a winding sheet and laid out on a wooden board for the lykewake. All the mirrors in the castle were covered. She sent a servant out to tell the bees that Quincey was dead.

I never understood her ways as a child, her stories of ghosts and goblins frightened me. I thought it nothing but foolish superstition. Hocus pocus and humbug. I never knew that I was the fool.

There are a hundred pairs of antlers on the walls of the hunting hall. Quincey would wake early, before dawn, for a day of stalking. We trudged uphill, through rough heather and icy mists. He was a fine student, listening intently to every word the ghillie said.

It was a far cry from hunting buffalo: firing a Winchester as you rode high in the saddle, among the stampeding herd. Highland stalking is a quiet pursuit. Whispers and footfalls. Taking a stag with a single shot.

Quincey's first stag was a twelve pointer. The ghillie told him how best to clean the beast. Quincey insisted on gralloching the

stag with his Bowie knife, bleeding it out, and cutting its in-
testines and stomach from the carcass.

The antlers from Quincey's stag hang in the hunting hall. He
lies beneath them, like a Viking hero, bound for Valhalla.

Pocket notebook of Professor Abraham Van Helsing

22 November

Madam Blacklunans is a most extraordinary woman.

She tells me that she is descended from a wizard, the infamous Earl of Glenshee. He was an astrologer, and dabbler in
alchemy and sorcery, an associate of the unfortunate Lady
Glamis.

Janet Douglas, Lady Glamis, was an accused poisoner, tried
for attempting to murder King James VI. She was burned at the
stake as a witch, in Edinburgh, on Castle Hill.

I have no doubt that if Euphemia, Lady Blacklunans, was a
subject of King James, she would suffer a similar fate.

Her library is most remarkable. It is well stocked with books
of the occult and the dark arts. There is both the original French
and English translation of 'Traité sur les apparitions des esprits et
sur les vampires ou les revenans de Hongrie, de Moravie, &c.'
Treatise on the Apparitions of Spirits and on Vampires or
Revenants of Hungary, Moravia, et al. by Abbot Antoine Au-
gustin Calmet, published 1746.

She has a fine collection of American Dime Novels, gifted by
Mr. Morris, and Penny Dreadfuls from London. The shelves hold
Sweeney Todd the Demon Barber, *Hurricane Nell the Girl Dead-
Shot*, *Varney the Vampire*, *Spring-heeled Jack*, *Calamity Jane*, and
Buffalo Bill.

Dr. Seward's Diary

24 November

Quincey Morris was buried today, in the small graveyard by

the chapel, in the grounds of Blacklunans Castle.

The funeral was almost pagan in nature. Quincey was buried with cigars and a bottle of single-malt Scotch whisky. Arthur placed Quincey's Bowie knife in the coffin. Mrs. Harker has promised to plant a hawthorn tree over the grave in the spring.

Unexpectedly we had a visitor from Balmoral. Princess Beatrice arrived by coach, veiled and dressed in mourning clothes.

She carried a letter from Queen Victoria. We are to ride north, for a private audience with Her Majesty.

By Royal Command.

Journal of Arthur Holmwood, Lord Godalming

25 November

It is no small thing to meet the Queen.

Her Majesty appeared quite frail, her hand trembling as we sat to tea. She told us how sorry she was to hear of Quincey's passing. She did not speak Dracula's name, but she had been told of his deeds and how he was destroyed.

Princess Beatrice took Jack, Harker, Mina, and I to tour the castle's ballroom, as the Queen met in private with my mother and Professor Van Helsing.

I recall the Queen's parting words: 'Grief can make one do such frightful things.'

Dr. Seward's Diary

26 November

I never thought to see such things, to keep such secrets.

A little after dawn we took a carriage to Glamis Castle. Van Helsing, Arthur, Harker, Mina, and I.

Van Helsing sat, grim faced and silent.

'What you will see this day, must never be revealed.' The professor finally said. 'The mystery of Glamis. This secret will become your burden.'

Glamis Castle was all but deserted. A skeleton crew of servants remained. The ghillie showed us to the kitchens, where the door was barred and barricaded shut.

'It is the Monster of Glamis, you see.' Van Helsing told us. 'The Queen, Madam Victoria, has commanded that we end it, so it will not take another innocent life.'

Van Helsing ordered the ghillie and the servants to stack and light a pyre out in the courtyard.

'Lord Godalming, if you please.' Van Helsing said. 'Prepare your rifle.'

Arthur cradled Quincey's Winchester in his arms.

Harker and I dismantled the makeshift barricade and kicked open the doors. The smell of filth and burned flesh was overwhelming.

A crooked, wretched thing bent over the kitchen hearth, singing to itself. It had murdered a young maidservant, dragged her body to the kitchens and impaled her on an iron spit. She slowly roasted above the fire.

'Arthur,' Van Helsing whispered. 'Aim well.'

The monstrosity sniffed the air, staring, rheumy eyed.

I recognised its face, under the smeared blood and tattered hair.

It was Albert of Saxe-Coburg-Gotha. Prince Albert, the dead husband of Queen Victoria. Grieved over some thirty years. Un-Dead.

Arthur took the shot.

The bullet blew a hole in the monster's chest. Its ribcage exploded; heart pulped to raw meat. Prince Albert fell to the kitchen flagstones.

'Jack,' Van Helsing barked a command. 'I need you to cut off its head.'

I did not question. The professor handed me a gralloching knife and I hacked through throat, muscle and spine. Shifting to a small axe for chopping firewood as I needed.

'And dismember the cadaver.'

I took the limbs from the body. The ghillie returned and we wrapped the pieces of the dead prince in bed linens. We cast him to the flames.

Arthur never knew that his mother inherited a talent for necromancy. Aog-dhruidheachd they call it in Scots Gaelic, 'death or ghost sorcery.'

It was Lady Blacklunans who raised Victoria's dead husband from the grave. By Royal Command. Thirty years it was walled up, a dreadful secret, the Monster of Glamis Castle.

Mina said a prayer as we watched it burn.

Mark Oxbrow is a storyteller, author and ghostwriter. His short story, 'White as Snow, Red as Blood' was published by *Dracula Beyond Stoker*, accompanying Issue One. His story 'No Doves Come from Raven's Eggs,' was recommended by legendary editor Ellen Datlow as one of the best horror short stories of the year. Mark's books feature ghost stories, witch goddesses, Arthurian legends, poison gardens, folk horror, medieval monsters and secret treasures. Mark was born and raised in Edinburgh, the world's most haunted city. Over twenty-five years ago, he founded Scotland's largest Halloween festival.

Punch
By Doris V. Sutherland

I shall maintain to my dying day that, of all the gentlemen's clubs in London, the one to house the most interesting set of members is the Windham Club. I am biased, of course, as I myself once belonged to that club; yet I feel no regret at not having instead joined one of the other, better-known clubs. Yes, it was Boodle's that played host to Gibbon, who doubtless fascinated his fellow members with talk of Rome's rise and fall; and certainly, White's boasted such military figures as Major-General Churchill and such men of letters as Colley Cibber. But as far as the Windham Club is concerned, I need not reach back into that previous century of Gibbon and Churchill and Cibber to find esteemed members: my contemporaries were quite sufficient. To illustrate this point, I need only recount the case of William Holmwood.

One day, in the year of our Lord 1861, the club's present membership had been tallied at 599. This meant that there was space for one more member, and I had the opportunity to nominate a gentleman whom I deemed worthy. In weighing the merits of numerous acquaintances, I began to reminisce about gentlemen whom I had known since my youth, among them William Holmwood. While I had encountered him only infrequently in recent years, I remembered well our time together as school-friends.

When I suffered the ordeals of my boyhood, Billy had always been on hand to tend to the bruises inflicted by my classmates and the burns of our teachers' candles. He also provided more stimulating conversation than any other lad in the school. The son of the fourth Earl of Godalming, he regaled me with many a tale of his aristocratic family. He made the Holmwoods sound as romantic as figures from the Matter of Britain (a subject which, incidentally, fascinated him: he vowed that his first child would be called Guinevere if a girl, Arthur if a boy). He would make a perfect member.

There was one small hindrance, however. As per the club's rules, my proposal needed to be seconded by another Windham gentleman. While a few members were former schoolmates of mine, none could recall William. I was prepared to accept that, among all of the club members, I was alone in knowing this most redoubtable young man, when I was approached by R. M. Renfield, a quiet fellow whom we knew affectionately as Rennie.

"I say, old boy, I couldn't help but hear you asking about William Holmwood."

Hearing my friend's name took me by surprise. "Why, did you know him?"

Renfield revealed that he'd first met my old schoolchum at Epsom, on a Derby day some years ago. At that point he began providing a detailed account of that particular Derby and listing the various attendees; evidently a devotee of Darwin, Renfield made a careful arrangement of these creatures into a sort of evolutionary scale, with H.R.H. the Prince of Wales at the top and the dog that ran into the racecourse at the bottom. I had to offer a firm reminder that he was meant to be informing me about William.

"Oh, yes, well. I gather that Mr. Holmwood concocted the recipe for the burnt rum punch which we enjoyed that Derby night. Come the following years, that punch became almost as much a Derby fixture as the Aunt Sally or the minstrels."

It sounded plausible that the man described was indeed my friend. William had a flair for unusual beverages, and it made sense that he would be an avid derby-goer, Epsom being not so far from his family estate in Surrey.

I no longer had William's address, but after following my wider London social circle, I was able to meet someone who could arrange a reunion. Finally, I had the pleasure of inviting Billy for tea. This was where I told him all about the Windham Club.

"I must say," William remarked, "that these days, my mind has been occupied less with London and more with the Surrey countryside, and I rather miss the days when I made proper acquaintances in the city. This club of yours sounds a fine proposition indeed."

I remember well the day in which I first escorted my old friend William Holmwood into the Windham, where we found those present in a state of overall despondency.

"You must remember," I said to William, "that the Windham is primarily a literary club. Your new companions shall be mostly men of letters."

He gave a nod of understanding. I could tell that he was cataloguing a mental bookshelf in preparation for when the conversations began. And begin they did—but not in the way that I had hoped.

William raised Croker's three volumes of Irish fairy legends, but this led only to a most tedious discourse around the recent founding of the Irish Republican Brotherhood. Next, he mentioned the ongoing scholarly dispute over the manuscript unearthed by Horace Walpole regarding a haunted castle (did the events occur at Italy's Otranto or Bohemia's Otrhany?) which merely split the conversation between those interested in Italy's tiresome slog towards independence, and those who, for reasons I can hardly guess at, wished to discuss the place of the Czech peoples in the Austrian Empire! As for my friend's remarks on the relative merits of Ackerbarth and Thorpe's renditions of Beowulf, these prompted only witless stares.

I was astonished that, save for Rennie, none of my peers grasped just what an engaging individual I had ushered into their presence. Why, William's encyclopaedic knowledge of haunted buildings alone surely made him the most fascinating Windham member since Major General Churchill perished at Maharajpore.

"Men of letters they may well be," said William. "But not quite the same letters with which I concern myself."

"These fools do not appreciate you," I said to him.

Renfield was standing next to William, and of the two, was rather shorter. They reminded me of those Medieval illustrations in which the nobility towered above the commoners. I was heartened that Rennie appeared to be as scandalised as I: "But Mr. Holmwood's the son of an Earl," he proclaimed. "What more could they ask?"

William smiled and uttered one of those little jokes that he never failed to conjure on the spur of the moment.

"Perhaps an Earl."

We shared a laugh, marking us as three friends in what may as well have been a pool of strangers.

"I tell you what," said William at long last, "perhaps you two gentlemen might care to join me at the family home in Godalming."

N ever before or since have I visited a place quite so steeped in legend as Godalming and its surrounding area. The region is a veritable whirlpool of the imagination.

A little over six miles to the southwest of Godalming is Thursley, a village named after the pagan deity Thunor, or Thor. The nearby Thunder Hill and Hammer Ponds testify to the lingering memory of this thunder-god and his implement of choice. Further south and near the outskirts of Surrey we find the Devil's Jumps, three hills that loom over the sandy heath; their monicker evidently dates from after the Christianisation of the English. In short, my friend lived in a stretch of country where past generations had imagined Satan and Thor and God knows how many other marvellous figures striding across the landscape.

Of all the place-names around Godalming, the most intriguing is the Devil's Punchbowl. Located between Thursley and the Devil's Jumps, the so-called Punchbowl is a vast hollow whose steep walls afford a picturesque view. The monicker must be comparatively recent, unless we are to suppose our Saxon forebears hardy enough to have procured punch from the Indies. How and why did it get its name? What imagination could, upon looking out at that natural formation, visualise it as the drinking-vessel of Beelzebub himself? Such questions engaged my mind as I enjoyed the Surrey landscape.

This, of course, was when Renfield and I paid William Holmwood a visit at Godalming Manor, and our mutual friend took us on a trudge in the surrounding country. We passed through a place called Peper Harrow, a name that William informed us meant Piper's Temple; doubtless, this was once a site of pagan import. Our journey concluded in Mother Ludlam's Hole, a modest cave purportedly inhabited, in years past, by a witch.

"My grandmother spoke of this place," said William, his voice echoing across the cave walls. "In her day, there were chairs to sit on. Cups, too, so you could take a drink from Mother Ludlam's magic stream. All gone, now, I fear."

"And considering what Monsieur Pasteur's been telling us about germs, good riddance," said Clara.

Ah, yes, I suppose that I should introduce Clara.

Clara was William's fiancée and the daughter of Lord Lovel, and I confess to finding her both charming and aggravating. Her line had many intriguing tales of family hauntings, going all the way back to the reign of Henry VI, but she had little interest in discussing that sort of thing. A close childhood friend of hers, the granddaughter of Lord Byron, had introduced her to sundry forms of mathematics and engineering which had supplanted romantic poetry in that family's interests: difference engines and analytical engines and other such notions that, I admit, made my head spin.

Clara's interjections did much to colour our trip. When William spoke of a lady of the sixteenth century, Agnes Waters, who pleaded guilty to the bewitching of bullocks, Clara turned the conversation away from witchcraft and towards the torture of women and the madness of crowds. She preferred physics to spirits and no doubt considered Poe's thousand-and-second Arabian Night greater than any true composition by Scheherazade. That a man as romantic as William Holmwood should choose so profane a lady confounded me.

Once the jaunt was over, William gave a guided tour of Godalming Manor. He showed us the portraits of his ancestors, going all the way back to the first Earl of Godalming, Edward Holmwood. It was he who purchased the manor in 1726 from the old family that had constructed it around two and a half centuries beforehand. There were four such portraits, the most recent being William's father. When the time came for Billy to inherit the peerage and become the fifth Earl of Godalming, he, too, would have his picture added to the row.

After admiring the portrait of the present Lord Godalming, a man of bushy moustaches and gleaming medals, I asked William of his father's present whereabouts.

"Father is in India still. But with the sepoy rebellion quashed, his time as Lieutenant-General is surely peaceful. He should be home before long."

"What a delight for him to meet his future daughter-in-law," I exclaimed.

Here, William became quite agitated, and I was struck with embarrassment: I had evidently touched upon a matter of some tenderness. Then, smiling, my friend apologised.

"I fear that we Holmwoods have something of a family superstition concerning marriage."

I begged him to go into more detail about this tantalising subject; and once again, I found my vote being seconded by Ren-

nie. His agitation replaced with good humour, William sat down
to explain.

Many a distinguished family has stories concerning
omens of death. In Ireland, it is said that when the
present Viscount Goremanston lies dying, foxes shall gather at the
family castle. The Oxenham family of Devon is purportedly
haunted by the apparition of a white bird that manifests whenev-
er a member passes on. In Scotland, the Kinchardine clan has its
Lham-dearg, or Spectre of the Bloody Hand: a phantom soldier
that appears with a challenge to combat. Sir Walter Scott recounts
how this particular spook fought with three brothers in 1669, a
conflict which the brothers did not survive. (This tale raises a
question akin to Plutarch's old chestnut of the chicken and the
egg: how many such omens merely signify doom, and how many
are active agents of death?)

In the case of the Holmwood dynasty, the superstition is as
follows: the present Lord Godalming is doomed to perish shortly
after his eldest son, the heir to the title, finds a lady to wed.

Weeks after William's parents had first married, his grandfather Charles—the third Earl of Godalming—fell from one of the
great chalk-cliffs of the North Downs and smashed asunder on
the ground below. Most ascribed his death to an unfortunate accident, although malicious tongues wagged that Charles was filled
with shame at his son marrying Anna di Vivaldi, a lady from a
somewhat disreputable Neapolitan family. The surviving Holmwoods blamed the curse. Charles' father Philip, the second Earl of
Godalming, had died from a sickness that (according to persistent
rumours) resulted from poisoning. This occurred the day after
Charles married Lady Kelnor of Drumer, whose family penchant
for elaborate games earned it a reputation for frivolity. The sorry
saga appears to have begun with Edward Holmwood, the first
Earl of Godalming, who died in 1764. This doomed Earl's newly
acquired daughter-in-law was Elizabeth Murgatroyd, whose family was purportedly cursed by a witch. Once again, the dubious
reputations of these various ladies and the conceivably self-in-

flected dooms of their husbands rather make one contemplate
matters of ovation amongst poultry.

T ime passed, and Renfield and I paid many more visits
to the Godalming estate until we had the pleasure of
meeting William's father, Lord Godalming. The old gent had giv-
en one last review of the Eleventh Hussars in India and finally
retired from the army. He was doubtless eager to spend his remaining years regaling his English household with tales of the
great mutiny.

A servant poured us wine. "I promise that you shall try my
burnt rum punch someday," said William, "but today is not quite
the occasion."

Lord Godalming, sure enough, had plenty of stories. He had
been Lieutenant-General in the Eighth King's Royal Irish Hussars
those selfsame men responsible for slaying the Rani of Khansi: the
Raja's widow, a veritable Eastern Boadicea. His military rise had
started from his time as a humble Lieutenant-Colonel, a rank he
had earned with the princely sum of £35,000. ("I rather fear," he
said, "that in a few years' time, they shall have ended such prac-
tices, and I weep for the young men who must follow less noble
paths to glory.")

I sipped my wine, wondering how it might compare with
that fabled punch. His Lordship continued.

"The rajah in Nahdoor had assembled an army to wipe out
the infidels and capture our women. Arisings in Lucknow and
Cawnpore, you know. Every Englishman in India broke into a
cold sweat, nobility and ruffians alike! But we stood firm, band-
ing our troops together…"

He then began rattling off a seemingly interminable list that
included the Seventy-fifth Regiment, the First Bengal Fusiliers,
various newly-raised irregular horses and who knows what else.

"I tell you," he said, "when I looked out at Delhi from the
great ridge, I felt pride at seeing our towers fully armed. No, there
was not a chance of us surrendering that noble city. When our
men marched into battle, they bellowed out: 'Remember the

ladies!'" (He slammed a fist on the table, rattling cutlery.) "'Remember the children!'" (Plates were sent quivering.) "'Remember Lucknow and Cawnpore!'" (A bottle of wine leapt upwards.)

A servant handed Lord Godalming a handkerchief. He nodded in gratitude before mopping the sweat from his brow. His breath regained, he continued.

"The Union Jack flew again above the palace of Delphi when all was said and done, but it was a terrible business. And to think, it all started with a false rumour that we English were greasing rifle cartridges with pigs' fat. An affront to their religion, you know. Hurrumph! These heathen ways!"

"I would be careful about saying that, Father," remarked William. "There is truth in many a fable, including the fables of foreign climes."

Clara laughed. "You always were a superstitious man, Billy."

"And you a modern, material-minded sort, Clara." William spoke with a wry smile but an earnest look in his eyes. "Some of us, however, are attuned to spiritual matters."

Clara had not yet finished her philosophical coquetry. "My dear Will, given the stock you place in these quaint old notions, surely you must find yourself tempting fate by promising our guests rum punch so close to the Devil's own punchbowl?"

I believe that a sharp intake of breath was shared by all of the gentlemen present. Seldom had I seen an individual's manliness so challenged by his lady-love. William replied in a jaunty air:

"You are quite right, dear Clara. And to prove that I have no fear, tonight I shall brew a burnt rum punch in the very middle of the Devil's Punchbowl."

That night, we set up a campfire with stones and kindling in the Punchbowl's centre. No servants were there; no Clara or Lord Godalming. Just William, Rennie and myself. Suspended above our fire was a wooden pole, from which dangled a large bowl of bubbling water.

Flames danced in William's eyes as he recited those infamous words:

"Double, double, toil and trouble, fire burn and cauldron bubble."

As he reached into a basket containing his ingredients, he began improvising his rhyme:

"Sicilian lemons in a pair, rub their skins at Satan's lair."

The lemons he held were large and juicy-looking, their rinds pleasingly rough. He continued:

"From the Indies' harvests humble, lumps of sugar, white and crumbled."

Renfield held up the conical loaf of sugar. It was my job to wield the iron sugar-nips, with which I clipped off some generous lumps. These tumbled into a second bowl, sitting by the fire. Renfield helped as William rubbed the chipped-off sugar against the lemon-rinds until it absorbed the citrus juice. In a typical punch recipe, more sugar would be added at this point. Yet William had wrapped up the sugarloaf: this would be a sour punch indeed.

"Peel of orange, grown in Seville, bitter flavours for the Devil!"

William spoke these words as I unwrapped a bundle of orange peel, which I placed with the sugar in the smaller bowl. William squeezed the lemons over the sugar and peels, while Renfield used a thin pestle to mix and bruise the concoction. All the while, the large bowl was bubbling over the fire.

"Water that has reached the boil atop the Devil's own dark soil!"

I helped as William poured boiling water from the large bowl into the smaller vessel, where Renfield mixed it up. William then placed a large sieve over the bubbling bowl, and together, we poured the sugary mixture into the boiling liquid. Next, he added the dark and pungent contents of a rum-bottle to the brew.

"Plantations gave us rum from far, now taste the air of the midnight hour!"

My next job was to contribute a quart of porter. William continued his amusing incantation.

"With porter brewed in London town, we toast his most infernal crown!"

The final ingredient was a dash of cold water from a bottle. After a stir, the brew was served. We each took a glassful of the Devil's punch.

I took my first sip. The flavour of the rum and porter were altogether subtler than expected. The sharpness of the lemon and the bitterness of the orange would have been enough to subsume those ingredients, but there was another flavour which seemed oddly familiar. It reminded me of a boyhood incident in which I first tasted coffee, sipped secretly from my father's mug, and striking my childish and unprepared palette as a taste drawn from the earth itself. This Devil's Punch had the same quality, and left my head in a haze.

"Well," I remarked, "I dare say you would never find this drink at White's or Boodles!"

William was as modest as ever. "Those clubs must have the finest vintage of wines in store."

"Common fare for common people," I replied. I then noticed how silent Rennie had been.

I looked up at him, and saw movement flicker across the glass in his hand. It was a spider; no, more than one! The entire glass was crawling with them! I was about to alert him, when to my utter disgust, he rubbed the glass to pick up a few of the spiders along his finger, which he then inserted into his mouth.

I looked away in revulsion, and my eyes fell upon William. Yet the man before me was no longer a man: he a was a painting. His entire form, from his clothes to his skin, stood out from the darkness like richly-pigmented oil paints. I could even see the texture of the brushstrokes. Rather than his simple hiking attire of only a minute prior, he was clothed in the formal dress that a titled gentlemen might wear when sitting for his portrait.

The strokes of paint that made up his face distorted as his brow furrowed and his lips moved.

"Are you quite alright, old boy?"

I rubbed my thumb and forefinger over my eyes. When I looked again, both visions had faded. Renfield, his clean glass shimmering in the firelight, showed no indication of having swallowed a mouthful of arachnids; he merely gazed at me with silent concern. As for William Holmwood, he was no more than a handsome man dressed for a countryside trip.

"Strong drink," I replied.

We sat in silence. I quaffed the last of my punch while Renfield finished his. I then noticed that William had not taken a single sip from his glass: it was still full, and had been through our entire conversation.

"Is your stomach voicing disagreement?" I asked.

He shook his head. "I am thinking less of my stomach and more of my soul. Clara may scoff, but…." He tossed the contents of the glass into the undergrowth.

"Bit of a waste," I murmured.

"Think of it as an offering to whatever pagan deity inhabits this place," said William.

Renfield grinned. "Are you rendering unto Satan that which is Satan's?"

William did not return the smile.

We were staying at the house for a week or so, and every afternoon, Lord Godalming would entertain us with yet another tale of the Fourth Sikh Infantry or the Ghoorka Kumaan battalion or somesuch. My sleep, meanwhile, was fitful.

Each night I was haunted by visions of William as I saw him at the Punchbowl: that living portrait, that gentleman of immortal pigments. Sometimes he towered above the Surrey landscape, a Titan every bit the match of Thor or Satan. Other times he strode his majestic form into the Windham Club, its members kneeling in reverence to the fifth Earl of Godalming. Still other nights gave me the simple and wholly achievable image of William's portrait hanging there in his home, alongside the likenesses of his departed ancestors.

Each time I would awake with a conviction in my mind, one that strengthened with every successive dream. I knew full well that it was my duty to ensure my friend's rightful ascension. I had merely to carry out a small act and make a certain sacrifice.

O n the final night, when all others had gone to sleep and I was confined to my guest bedroom, I decided to commence my plan.

I pulled off the bedsheet and draped it around my form. I took a length of cheesecloth that I had purloined earlier and wrapped it around my face; it was thin enough to allow me to see and to breathe but, as I confirmed before the mirror, not so thin that my features would be recognisable. Finally, I removed a pillowcase and turned it into a makeshift hood. Were I appearing onstage as Hamlet's father I would have been a laughing stock, but I held hope that the mansion's darkness would work to my benefit.

As quietly as I could, I entered the hallway and headed to the adjacent guest bedroom in which Lord Godalming was quartered. I pushed the door open. There was no sound, no movement to be glimpsed in the shadows, and I knew that his Lordship was asleep. I tip-toed forwards until I was close enough to tug his blanket inch by inch.

There were many things that could yet go wrong. What if he awoke with a shout and alerted other sleepers? What if he saw through my disguise?

Instead, he sat up with a snorting gasp and gazed at me in silent horror. What little light had entered the room glimmered on his rheumy eyes.

"Lord Godalming, oh Lord Godalming," I said to him.

I did my best to approximate a soft, feminine voice, partly to ensure that I was quiet enough to avoid disturbing the other residents. Also, given my rather lithe and not-exactly-tall build, I reasoned that he might take me for a female spook. Which female spook, I cannot say. The witch responsible for his ancestors' curse? The spectre of Mother Ludlam? The vengeful spirit of the Rani of Khansi? But all that mattered was that he did not recognise me as one of the gentlemen lodged in the family manor.

His response was another gasp, this time mingled with a gurgle. To my relief, he refrained from calling out as he scrambled for the exit. I had left a wide berth between myself and the door so as not to discourage his flight. While he commenced his ungainly stumble through the doorway and into the corridor beyond, I pursued with a series of long and (I hoped) ethereally graceful strides.

I had trouble believing my luck as he reached the main stairwell without so much as raising his voice. However, events took a more foreboding turn when he headed towards the servants' quarters, evidently hoping to rouse somebody. What! This was not what I wanted! I lengthened my steps to overtake the aged oaf. I leapt in front of him and he halted before staggering backwards straight towards the stairs.

That, dear reader, is precisely what I desired.

I forced my visage into a lunatic grin which (I hoped) could be seen below the cheesecloth.

"I have come for you, Lord Godalming," I said in a falsetto tone. "Many years have passed but I came for you in the end!"

He was still staggering backwards and began shaking his head, his lips moving in a remonstration that emerged only as a low gibber. Guilt blanched his face; he clearly saw me as somebody from his past, although I can hardly say whom. I stepped towards him and he stepped backwards until, finally, he reached the stairs and tumbled downwards.

His yell was cut off when his head collided with a step halfway down. From then on, the only sounds he made were the regular thuds and one or two cracks resulting from various parts of his anatomy colliding with the staircase.

I waited to see if the noise had awoken any other members of the household. But there were no footsteps, no creaking of doors. I was safe.

I descended the stairs and inspected Lord Godalming, who was sprawled out with a pool of dark blood spilling from the back of his head and a look of abject terror upon his lifeless face. I admit, I had rather hoped him to live long enough to tell of my ghostly presence. Then, a stroke of inspiration hit me. I took his late Lordship's hands beneath my own and manipulated them, rending his nightshirt open. From there, I commenced using his own hands to tug and tear at his underthings. Once his grey-haired chest, his rotund paunch and his masculine organ were all exposed, he looked the very image of a man who had simply lost his mind in the middle of the night.

I must have been grinning still as I ascended the stairs and returned to my guest bedroom.

My sleep was restless, in the manner of an eager schoolboy the night before a lavish house party. I awoke just as the birds were beginning to sing, and I listened to the rest of the household awaken in their usual manner around me. I heard doors opening, feet scurrying, words of greeting. Then, somebody saw the stairwell. Whether it was Clara or one of the maids I cannot say, although the scream was most assuredly feminine.

I dashed from the bedroom, feigning the utmost concern. By that time, everybody was up and about: William, Clara, the servants, even Renfield. The only person not stampeding in dismay was the late Lord Godalming.

T he wedding came soon after the wake. As is to be expected, any joviality was tempered by gloomier feelings. I caught sight of Clara, the new Lady Godalming, indulging in a morose chat with sallow-faced friends. I was some distance away, but I swear that she uttered these words: "And to think, had I chosen another man, poor Billy's father would yet be alive!"

These sentiments struck me as perplexingly contrite. Many ladies would have given much to become wife to the fifth Earl of Godalming. But then, I have never quite grasped the feminine mind. As for myself, I was very much looking forward to arriving at the Windham Club with my old friend, the new peer!

S o concludes this confession, if the term fits. To me, a confession implies a degree of shame and a desire for candour, and I possess neither. I have no intention of publishing this document, and expect it to be found when I am long since dead and buried—if at all.

Why, then, did I write it?

The answer is simple. Now that you have read my testimony, you must surely agree with me that, of all the gentlemen's clubs to be found in London, the one to house the most interesting set of members is the Windham Club.

Smitten
By Henry Herz

Ray adopted a tactical stance, his left foot inches ahead of his right, and his shoulders square to the shooting range target twenty-five yards away. He emptied the fifteen-round magazine of his Glock in seconds, half the shots piercing the head, and the other half piercing the upper torso of the target.

Private detective work unavoidably involved boring tasks like paperwork and long hours of surveillance. However, the kind of cases DNR Investigative Services pursued could accelerate with little warning from dull to deadly. Hence the need to stay in shape and keep his combat skills sharp—commitments the six-foot, two-hundred-pound former US Ranger took seriously.

DNR differed from other detective agencies in several respects. First, it boasted only two employees, Ray and his boss, the owner. Second, rather than being headquartered in a rented office building in a low-rent part of town, DNR was based in the owner's sprawling, walled estate on the western edge of New York's Black River Wild Forest. Third, the firm didn't advertise publicly. Fourth, DNR paid its employees well. Very well. Fifth, as one might deduce from the prior three items, the owner was obscenely wealthy.

Monday morning, Ray arrived at his oak-paneled 'office,' a repurposed bedroom in his boss's sixteen-room mansion. Ray's reddish blond hair was cropped short, and he wore a bespoke dark blue suit with a blood red silk tie. His boss expected punctilious grooming and attire. Ray was unshakably loyal, and in any event, what the boss wanted, the boss got. Always.

Ray unbuttoned his jacket, sat at his mahogany desk, and checked the schedule for the day's first task. The words "client invoicing" stared back from his laptop as if mocking him.

He sighed. A tedious but necessary task.

Forty-five minutes of mind-numbing accounting work later, the ring of his office phone provided a welcome interruption. As DNR's number was unlisted, the only callers were clients, referrals from clients, or robocalls.

Standing to stretch his back, he took that call. "DNR Investigative Services. Ray speaking. How may we help you?"

"Good morning," replied a man in Received Pronunciation, the poshest of British accents. "My name is Thomas Christine. I seek your firm's assistance in locating a missing person."

Ray sat in his black and onyx Herman Miller Aeron desk chair and opened a client intake form on his computer. "We have experience in that regard. May I ask you some questions?"

"Of course."

"How did you find out about DNR?"

"Via referral." Mr. Christine paused. "But I would prefer not to say from whom."

Ray took note of that on the intake form. "I see. Did the police turn up anything regarding the missing person?"

A pause. "I have not requested their help." Christine cleared his throat. "This is a most unusual and, shall we say, delicate matter."

"I see." Delicate matters often proved to be the most interesting and lucrative cases. Ray collected the man's contact information. "Can you email us a photo of the missing person?"

Christine sighed. "I regret that I have no photo, but I can describe her. She is a nineteen-year-old woman, slender and demure, with long blonde hair and pale blue eyes. She speaks with a British accent."

Ray took notes. "Got it. Where did you last see her?"

"In London, but I subsequently traced her to the eastern United States. There, the trail went cold." Christine chuckled without mirth. "I do not know her date of birth, nor any of her government identification numbers. No driver's license number. No passport number. The dearth of information is why I need help from a company of DNR's vaunted reputation."

"We do our best. And the lady's name?"

The man spoke the lady's name and Ray's heart pounded as recognition struck him like a punch to the face.

Christine cleared his throat. "The matter is of such importance to me that I will pay double your customary rates."

Ray's eyebrows rose. DNR's customary rates were already exorbitant. They could afford to be very selective when taking on new clients. "I'll convey all this to my boss. He decides which cases we accept. I expect to get back to you later today."

"Thank you, Ray."

After hanging up, Ray attempted to run a check on Christine's phone number, but it did not show up in any of the databases he used. A quick background check confirmed the man could pay DNR's fees. *Interesting.* He strode to the adjacent room featuring ebony board and batten paneling and an ornate stone fireplace. "I just got a call from a prospective client, sir."

His boss sat at a Brobdingnagian desk, dramatically framed by a floor-to-ceiling stained glass window depicting a dragon *rampant guardant*. Wearing a black suit and royal purple tie, the man's deep gray eyes suggested an age belied by his trim physique. "Tell me more, Ray." He gestured to a guest chair.

Ray sat. "A British man named Thomas Christine wants our help locating a missing person. He's willing to pay double our normal rates."

Nodding, his boss replied, "Is that so? Based on your facial expression, there is more to this tale."

"Yes, sir. He's looking for *Lucy Westenra*." The name, well-known to the boss as a century-old vampire, hung in the air with foreboding.

His boss's eyes widened. "My, my. That *is* interesting. Someone wants to find the vampire we captured eleven months ago for her good and the good of the general populace." He closed his eyes in thought for a moment.

"Decline the case, Ray, with the excuse that we are currently overbooked." He tilted his head. "As you know, she owes us a fateful decision in one month's time." He glanced at his platinum and black enamel Patek Philippe Calatrava wristwatch. "Speaking of time, excuse me, Ray, but I have a client call scheduled."

A week later, Ray engaged in another necessary but boring task—reviewing videos recorded remotely as part of DNR's ongoing cases where they monitored for supernatural occurrences. Camera footage from the open decks of Norsemen Cruise Line ships showed no evidence of passenger kidnappings. The Wallachian Imports warehouse in Rome, NY revealed no signs of new vampire activity. The private residence in Hampstead, MD was another matter. Infrared images from the previous evening showed someone skulking through the bushes and trees of the backyard.

Ray rushed into his boss's office. "Sir. Last night, someone seemed to be scouting the house where we're holding Lucy Westenra. Luckily, they didn't break in. Do you think it could be a vampire hunter?"

His boss steepled his fingers. "I have heard rumors that a Van Helsing descendant yet lives. Does the video offer a clear view of the person's face?"

"No, sir. Should I conduct a reconnaissance of the Westenra house tonight?"

"Most assuredly. This is an odd coincidence given the call we received last week."

Ray loaded a black canvas duffle bag with gear tailored for the night's anticipated activities—black clothing and night vision goggles. Then he added body armor and weapons. His personal philosophy, one which had kept him alive in a very dangerous line of work, was *chance favors the prepared.*

He drove a nondescript gray van with tinted windows the six and a half hours to Hampstead, MD, arriving at a Walmart parking lot around dinner time. He ate some energy bars and fruit, changed into a black sweatsuit, and read a few chapters of Patrick Rothfuss's *The Name of the Wind* to pass the time.

Waiting for pedestrian traffic to cease, at 11 p.m. Ray drove to a nearby suburb of acre-plus lots shaded by old oak and maple trees, parking two blocks from his destination. Tugging on a black knit beanie cap, Ray grabbed his duffle bag and slipped out of the van. He hurried noiselessly to an expansive, two-story red brick Georgian Revival with symmetrical white-framed windows.

Confirming no one else was taking a late-night stroll, Ray dashed into the thick bushes lining the property. From his duffle bag, he withdrew an AN/PVS-31 binocular night vision device, infrared camera, and his Glock 19. He maneuvered toward the rear left corner of the lot, where he had a view of both the rear and one side of the house. Ray settled into the darkness, motionless and almost invisible.

At 1:20 a.m., the sound of twigs snapping underfoot reached Ray's ears. A man emerged from the trees near the lot's right rear corner. Ray took infrared photos and noted the intruder's appearance.

Maybe five-foot-eight. Slightly bulging waistline. Trucker jacket, blue jeans, and running shoes. Middle-aged, balding, with light hair. Most significantly, a silver crucifix pinned to the front of his jacket. To Ray's well-trained eyes, the man moved across the well-manicured rear lawn without the grace or situational awareness of an experienced military operator. Ray assumed the zippered bag in the man's left hand contained lock picks or door breaching tools.

When the man reached the back door, about twenty yards away, Ray stood. "What do you think you're doing?"

The man froze for a moment, then eased around to face Ray, brandishing a folding clip point knife. "Back off." The tremor in his voice betrayed his fear.

Amateur. Ray shook his head. "I don't think so." He drew his Glock. "What is that saying about knifes and gun fights?"

The man turned and bolted for the street.

Realizing it wasn't advisable to chase a man dressed in regular attire down a residential street at night while he was clothed all in black and wearing a BNVD, Ray held his position and cursed. Plus, the man could scream for help at the top of his lungs, and that would bring private security or the police. Ray removed the BNVD, stuffed his gear into his duffel bag, and jogged to the van. He drove ten miles west, renting a room at the Days Inn in Westminster.

His boss answered the phone on the first ring, no trace of drowsiness in his voice. "Yes, Ray?"

Ray gave a brief report.

"Interesting. Did the intruder sound like Thomas Christine?"

"No, sir. He didn't have a British accent."

"Although we do not know if this man sought Lucy, she cannot be loosed to prey upon the innocent ever again. I think I shall drive to Hampstead in the morning. For now, get some rest, Ray."

The following afternoon, Ray and his boss, dressed in nondescript sweaters and slacks, used a key to enter the front door of the Hampstead home. Contrary to longstanding rumor, Lucy Westenra had escaped Abraham Van Helsing's attempt to stake her over a century prior. Eleven months ago, Ray and his boss had imprisoned the vampire to contemplate a momentous choice they offered her.

An inspection of the basement confirmed that she remained in her mahogany coffin. The arcane power of a wild rose branch atop the coffin prevented the vampire Lucy from rising without help. A locked chest freezer held the coffin, keeping it safe from the prying eyes of potential trespassers.

The pair made themselves comfortable in the living room featuring richly upholstered couches and travertine flooring. "Did the infrared images of the intruder I emailed you ring any bells, sir?"

"Sadly, I found no matches on any of our databases, Ray. It seems all we can do is wait and hope the man returns so I can question him."

"Sir, given my encounter with him, there's a good chance he'll stay away for a while, or come back with a more heavily-armed crew."

"Those are distinct possibilities, and require appropriate precautions from us. For one, we shall, dare I say it, *stake* out Lucy's house from within. We can access the exterior-facing security camera feeds on your tablet computer. We will rest during the day and remain awake at night. To avoid betraying our presence, we shall keep the window shutters closed and the lights off at night. Sooner or later, the man will return. I feel it."

T hree days and nights passed without incident. Ray and his boss passed the evenings working on DNR's other cases, to the extent allowed by their remote location. Despite being in the field, Ray failed to escape the drudgery of business paperwork. Still, Lucy's commodious and luxuriously appointed home proved a vast improvement over the prior night's motel.

At 2 a.m. on the fourth day, as Ray invoiced customers from the dining room, his boss angled a tablet computer for him to see. "Our middle-aged intruder has returned and approaches the rear door once again. Please subdue the fellow. I shall monitor the cameras for any other intruders while you do so."

Ray nodded. "The guy's determined. I'll give him that." He strapped on a Smith & Wesson Model 500 five-shot revolver, grabbed a taser from his ready bag, and slipped out the front door. Ray crept barefoot toward the man, whose attention was focused on picking the lock of the rear door.

Stopping at a distance of ten feet from the intruder, Ray fired the taser.

The man gasped, spasmed, and fell to the ground.

Ray rushed over, pulled a zip tie from his pocket, and bound the man's wrists behind his back. He added a gag to prevent any calls for help.

With his key, Ray unlocked the back door so he could drag the intruder inside for a more discrete interrogation. As he bent over to grab the man, vice-like grips seized both his biceps. Though a strong man, Ray struggled futilely. His anger mixed with embarrassment that someone managed to sneak up on him.

"Do not cry for assistance," whispered a man in Received Pronunciation British before spinning Ray to face him. He did this with unbelievable speed, reversing his grip on Ray's arms before the Ranger could react. "Do what I say and no harm will befall you."

"No yelling. Got it," replied Ray in an even voice, taking in a tall, handsome man with curly brown hair. A black leather duster wrapped the stranger's shoulders. This was one of those times where Ray would have much preferred the tiresome drudgery of invoicing clients. His breath caught at a sudden realization. The man's inhuman stealth, strength, and speed meant he was probably a vampire. He averted his eyes to avoid being charmed into submission. "Mr. Christine, I presume?"

The man smiled. "Oh, what a clever fellow you are, Mister…?"

"Renfield," replied his boss, who had materialized behind Christine with his cane sword drawn, the razor-sharp blade of which now rested on the back of the man's neck. "I assure you I am faster than you, Mr. Christine. So, do not think you can dart away before I take your head. Kindly release Ray so we can go inside and discuss matters in a more civilized manner."

"As you wish." Christine let go of Ray's arms but did not turn. "How did you know I had your man?"

"Surveillance cameras. Plus, we are both wearing tactical throat mic headsets, so I heard Ray stalling you. Well done, by the way."

"Thank you, sir." Ray opened the rear door, flicked on a light switch, and dragged the unconscious man into a spacious wallpapered kitchen, which included top-of-the-line stainless steel appliances, a waterfall Carrara marble counter, and four black leather bar stools.

Ray's boss and Christine followed, the former's sword never wavering from its threatening position against the latter's cervical spine.

"Please have a seat, Mr. Christine. Ray, cover him with your gun."

"Yes, sir." Ray leveled his pistol at Thomas's heart.

"Please do not try anything, Mr. Christine. We, too, have no wish to harm you, but know that Ray's revolver is loaded with magnum rounds of half-inch-diameter sharpened Brazilian olive wood. Two-thousand-feet per second stakes. Ray is quite the accurate shot, I should add." He returned his sword to its cane scabbard.

Christine turned to view his captor, jerking as if stung by a bee. "Dracula! After all these years!"

"Indeed. I am the D in DNR Investigative Services." As Dracula inspected the man's face, a smile brightening his countenance. "Well, this night is full of surprises, Mr. Christine…or, should I say, the honorable Arthur Holmwood, Lord Godalming?"

Ray's mouth fell open, but his aim remained steady. "What?"

Dracula nodded. "I am as perplexed as you, Ray. Would you kindly elaborate for us, Mr. Holmwood?"

Holmwood sighed. "After you turned Lucy into a vampire in London long ago, she was unable to control her hunger and did the same to me. At first, I grieved bitterly for my immortal soul. Eventually, I realized a fair price had been extracted in exchange for me spending eternity with my beloved." His eyes glistened. "Tragically, our time together was cut short, thanks to Abraham Van Helsing, curse his name. Failing to destroy you, he hunted Lucy. His pursuit forced us to separate. I lost contact with my beloved and have sought her all these long years. Is she here? Tell me it is so, I pray you."

Dracula nodded. "Even the undead can love. I have felt it myself." He grinned. "She is indeed here, nearing the completion of a twelve-month sentence."

"Sentence?"

"Tell him, Ray."

"Decades ago, my master summoned the will to control his impulses and to act for the benefit of humanity. He vowed to stop stalking strangers and draining their lifeblood. My master also insists that his vampire descendants do the same. I'm the latest generation in the line of faithful Renfields serving him. He sips my blood weekly, giving him the nourishment he needs, while leaving me human. When we found Lucy a year ago, she did not share his philosophy...and she fed on children." Distaste marred Ray's handsome face. "So, my master, acknowledging responsibility for making her a vampire, gave her a year to consider whether to follow his practice or to be staked."

Holmwood scowled. "That is not much of a choice. I reached the same conclusion long ago to save what I could of my soul. I vowed to only feed from willing thralls, and never enough to turn them."

"I prefer the title *assistant* to thrall," replied Ray, still brandishing his revolver. "And, no offense, but you could just be saying that so we let you go."

Holmwood stiffened. "I did not feed on you when I had the chance."

"True." Dracula placed a reassuring hand on Ray's shoulder. "And his claim is verified easily enough." He removed the gag from Holmwood's helper's mouth, gently shook him to consciousness, and assisted the man to a seat. He stared into the man's eyes, charming him into subservience. The man's face went slack. "What is your name?"

"David Larson."

"Tell me, Mr. Larson, of your master's feeding arrangements."

The man confirmed Holmwood's tale.

"Well, well." Dracula smiled. "This is an unexpectedly positive development. Who better than her fiancé to help Lucy acclimate to a new…lifestyle? One last precaution, though." He searched Larson for weapons, pocketing a knife and a SIG SAUER 1911 pistol.

"Mr. Holmwood, your arrival has accelerated our schedule by a month, but no matter. If, without knowing you are here, she vows to only feed off the willing, then I will be pleased to reunite you with your betrothed."

Holmwood's face lit up like a child's on Christmas morning. "To see her would be the first true joy I have experienced in over a century." Then worry marred his brow. "I pray she makes the right choice."

"As do I." Dracula nodded. "Excuse me while I speak with Lucy to learn her decision." He left the kitchen and descended into the basement.

Still pointing the revolver at Holmwood, Ray asked, "I'm curious how you found this address."

"My *assistant*, David, has great facility with computers. Last week, he found public records mentioning the sale last year of a Home Wood Estates by a Mrs. Lucretia Blueford. 'Home Wood' sounds like Holmwood, Lucretia could be a variant of Lucy, and Blueford could be a version of the title Hampstead, *England* children accorded her—Bloofer Lady. Any one of these could have been a coincidence, but taken together, the confluence seemed more than providential."

Ray nodded. "You're right." He rolled his shoulders to loosen some tension. "As you know, we're private investigators. What do you do for a living?"

"Ah, I specialize in arranging, shall we say, *discrete* transportation, for when someone wishes to travel or ship cargo without the knowledge of governmental agencies or publicly traded companies."

Ray filed away that valuable tidbit, as his master needed assistance on occasion when crossing bodies of water.

Holmwood's eyes snapped to the right at the sound of footsteps ascending the stairs from the basement.

Dracula, still out of sight, called ahead, "I have wonderful news. Lucy has agreed not to prey on the unwilling. Lucy, we have a guest you will be pleased to meet."

Holmwood stood, trembling with emotion at the long over-due reunion.

Dracula led Lucy into the room, her arm hooked through his like a father giving away the bride at a wedding.

Hair rumpled from eleven months in a coffin and eyes blinking in the glare of the kitchen lighting, Lucy nevertheless remained a stunning, slender blonde with pale blue eyes that went wide at the sight of her betrothed. Her mouth formed an 'o' of wonder. "Arthur! Can it be?"

Holmwood rushed into the arms of his beloved, who tucked her head at his collarbone, not to drink, but to inhale the scent of her man. He stroked her long hair. The pair swayed like a couple slow dancing.

Holmwood cradled her face in his hands, his thumb caressing her cheek, lost in her gaze. "Oh, Lucy! You are as beautiful as I remembered. How I have missed you."

"I feared I would never see you again, my dear Arthur." Lucy traced delicate fingertips over his tricep.

Tears rolled down their cheeks as they held the long-delayed embrace. Even Dracula and Ray's eyes glistened.

Holmwood eased his lips to Lucy's, offering a delicate kiss that was somehow both passionate and restrained.

"Would someone please untie me now?" asked Larson, provoking laughter. "I'm guessing I've got a wedding to arrange."

Author's Notes

This is the fifth adventure of occult detectives Dracula and Ray Renfield, whose covert exploits are documented in *Norsemen Cruise Line*, Dracula Beyond Stoker issue #1, *Don't Mess With a Renfield*, Dracula Beyond Stoker issue #2, *Loose End*, Dracula Beyond Stoker issue #3, and *Cold Shoulders*, Dracula Beyond Stoker issue #4.

DNR is a playful reference to Dracula & Renfield, as well as the medical term, "do not resuscitate."

Henry Herz has written for Daily Science Fiction, Weird Tales, Pseudopod, Metastellar, Titan Books, Highlights for Children, Ladybug Magazine, and anthologies from Albert Whitman, Blackstone Publishing, Third Flatiron, Brigids Gate Press, Air and Nothingness Press, Baen Books, and elsewhere. He's edited eight anthologies and written fourteen picture books.
www.henryherz.com

Dr. John Seward
The Voice of Reason
By Chris McAuley

Dr. John Seward stands as one of the most complex and intriguing characters in Bram Stoker's Dracula. A man of science and reason, Seward's role in the novel is pivotal, serving as a bridge between the rational world of Victorian medicine and the supernatural horrors that defy explanation. This essay delves into the character of Dr. John Seward, exploring his significance in the narrative, his symbolic role as a man of science, and his portrayal in various adaptations of Dracula.

Seward is introduced to readers as the head of a lunatic asylum, a position that immediately establishes him as a man of intellect and authority. Stoker paints him as a figure of rationality and discipline, dedicated to his work and deeply invested in the scientific method. He is a grounded, logical presence within the narrative, someone who seeks to understand the world through observation and analysis.

Throughout the novel, Seward's scientific approach is both a strength and a limitation. While his reliance on logic and reason allows him to contribute valuable insights, it also blinds him, at times, to the more fantastical elements of the events unfolding around him.

This reflects the broader tension in Victorian society between the advances of science and the persistence of superstition and the supernatural. Seward's struggle to reconcile these conflicting worldviews adds depth to his character, making him one of the most relatable figures in the novel. His skepticism and eventual acceptance of the supernatural forces at play in Dracula mirror the journey of many readers who, like Seward, must expand their understanding of the world to accommodate the inexplicable.

One of the most poignant aspects of Dr. Seward's character is his unrequited love for Lucy Westenra. Unlike Arthur Holmwood, who is engaged to Lucy, or Quincey Morris, whose love for her is more outwardly passionate, Seward's affection is quiet and reserved. His love for Lucy is deeply intertwined with his sense of duty and care for her well-being. As a doctor, he is committed to diagnosing and treating her mysterious illness, but as a man, he is torn by his feelings for her and the knowledge that she does not reciprocate them.

Seward's heartbreak over Lucy's decline is palpable. His scientific detachment crumbles as he watches her suffer, and his helplessness in the face of her illness is a source of profound frustration and sorrow. This emotional conflict humanizes Seward, revealing the vulnerability beneath his rational exterior. His love for Lucy is a driving force behind his actions throughout the novel, and it is this love that ultimately pushes him to join Van Helsing in the fight against Dracula.

Within the group of vampire hunters, Dr. Seward serves as a crucial link between the scientific world and the supernatural. His medical expertise and logical mind are invaluable, particularly in the early stages of the novel, when the group struggles to understand the nature of Lucy's illness. His detailed diaries and case notes provide a structured, methodical approach to the events, offering readers a window into the rational mind grappling with the irrational.

Seward's relationship with Professor Van Helsing is crucial to his development. As a former student of Van Helsing, Seward initially approaches the supernatural elements of the story with skepticism, relying on his scientific training to explain what he observes. However, under Van Helsing's guidance, he gradually opens his mind to the possibility that not everything can be explained by science alone. This intellectual journey is one of the most compelling aspects of Seward's character arc, as it showcases his willingness to adapt and learn, even when it challenges his fundamental beliefs.

Seward's position as the head of an asylum also plays a significant role in the group's efforts. His experience with mental illness gives him a unique perspective on the psychological impact of the events they face. This is particularly evident in his interactions with Renfield, a patient whose connection to Dracula becomes a key piece of the puzzle. Seward's professional relationship with Renfield provides insight into the broader themes of control, madness, and the influence of evil—an exploration that adds layers of complexity to the novel's narrative.

Dr. Seward's character serves as a symbol of the scientific advancements and the intellectual rigor of the late Victorian era. He represents the belief in progress and the power of reason to overcome challenges. However, Stoker also uses Seward to critique the limitations of science when confronted with the supernatural. Seward's journey from a man of pure reason to one who embraces the reality of the supernatural serves as a microcosm of the broader cultural shifts occurring during Stoker's time. The Victorian era was marked by significant advancements in science and technology, but it was also a period of spiritual and supernatural exploration. Seward's character embodies this duality, illustrating the struggle to reconcile empirical knowledge with the mysteries that lie beyond human understanding.

Dr. Seward's character acts as a foil to Count Dracula in several ways. While Dracula embodies the ancient, the mysterious, and the supernatural, Seward represents the modern, the rational, and the scientific. This contrast is central to the novel's exploration of the conflict between good and evil, knowledge and ignorance, life and death.

Seward's struggle to understand and combat Dracula mirrors the larger battle between the forces of reason and the unknown horrors that threaten to undermine it. As Seward moves from skepticism to belief, he symbolizes the journey of enlightenment, the recognition that there are forces in the world that defy simple categorization and demand a broader understanding.

The juxtaposition of Seward's clinical approach to life with Dracula's supernatural existence also highlights the limitations of human knowledge. Seward's reliance on science, while valuable, is ultimately insufficient to defeat the ancient evil that Dracula represents. This realization forces Seward to expand his worldview and embrace a more holistic approach, combining science with the wisdom and mysticism embodied by Van Helsing.

While Dr. Seward is a well-developed character, his portrayal in Dracula is not without its critiques. Some readers may find Seward's clinical detachment and methodical nature to be somewhat cold or distant, particularly in comparison to the more emotionally driven characters like Arthur Holmwood or Mina Harker. His scientific approach, while fascinating, can at times make him seem less relatable or sympathetic.

Moreover, Seward's character arc, while significant, is often overshadowed by the more dramatic transformations of characters like Jonathan Harker or Lucy Westenra. His role as the rational observer can sometimes place him in the background, making him more of a facilitator of the plot than a central figure driving it forward.

However, these critiques also underscore the unique position Seward occupies within the novel. His detachment and reliance on reason are not flaws but rather essential aspects of his character, reflecting the broader themes of the novel. Seward's journey is less about personal transformation and more about the intellectual and moral challenges that arise when the boundaries of knowledge are tested.

Dr. John Seward's character has been portrayed in various film and media adaptations of Dracula, each offering a different interpretation of his role in the story. In some adaptations, Seward is depicted as a strong, authoritative figure, emphasizing his scientific background and leadership qualities. In others, his character is merged with or overshadowed by other figures, reflecting the challenges of translating his complex role to the screen.

In the 1931 Universal Pictures adaptation of *Dracula*, Seward's character is present, but his role is significantly altered and reduced, with the focus shifting to other characters like Van Helsing and Harker. This trend continued in many early adaptations, where Seward was often depicted more as a background figure than a central character.

It wasn't until later adaptations, such as Francis Ford Coppola's *Bram Stoker's Dracula* (1992), that Seward began to receive more attention. As portrayed by Richard E. Grant, Seward is a troubled, passionate figure, deeply invested in the fight against Dracula and haunted by his unrequited love for Lucy. This version of Seward adds emotional depth to the character, emphasizing his internal conflicts and his gradual acceptance of the supernatural.

In television adaptations, Seward's character has been reinterpreted in various ways, sometimes emphasizing his scientific background, other times focusing on his emotional connections to the other characters. Each portrayal offers a different perspective on Seward's role in the narrative, highlighting the flexibility and complexity of his character.

Seward's legacy in *Dracula* is one of intellect, reason, and the pursuit of knowledge. He represents the rational mind confronting the inexplicable, a symbol of the Victorian belief in progress and the power of science. However, Seward's journey also serves as a reminder of the limitations of human knowledge and the need for humility in the face of the unknown.

Seward's character continues to resonate with readers and audiences because he embodies the struggle between reason and belief, science and superstition, sanity and madness. His role as a mediator between these worlds makes him a crucial figure in the Dracula narrative, one whose contributions are essential to the defeat of the ancient evil that threatens them all.

Seward's significance lies in his ability to adapt and learn, to expand his understanding of the world in the face of overwhelming evidence that challenges his fundamental beliefs. Through Dr. John Seward, Stoker explores the limits of science and reason, while also celebrating the courage to confront the unknown. As the rational mind of Dracula, Seward stands as a testament to the enduring power of knowledge, even when it is tested by the darkest of forces.

A Séance for Dr. Seward
By Jasmine De La Paz

On the outskirts of London, when the sun had long set and gas lamps burned to stave off the shadows, seven distinguished guests sat round a table in the manor of Lady Victoria White. Here, in a fine parlor suitable for society's elite, they welcomed the dark.

Diaphanous red sheets hung over lights like crimson ghosts. Thick velvet curtains blocked the soft rays of the waning moon, and shadows stretched below the dimmed chandelier. Each guest, corpse-like in this light, looked at Lady White with hungry hope.

Along with her guests, she too was in mourning. She sat straight-backed in a black gown made of lace; a matching choker wrapped around her long neck. Her golden hair, bright as the moon, contrasted with her gown and the scarlet gloom. Yes, she was a fine beauty—lips plump and pink as daises, pearly skin, and a voice that rang like an enchanting siren. Yet, despite her pleasing looks, one could look into her face no longer than a breath, for when her blue eyes met theirs, they felt a sinking sensation, as if her eyes alone brought forth all their buried secrets. There was *something* otherworldly about her stare. And that is why they trusted her as a medium—a spiritualist.

"We will begin," said Lady White, looking into each of their faces, "with a simple hymn. Please, let us hold hands." The flickering candles grew still, leaving lines of smoke shooting straight up from the flames and toward the heavens. The guests reached for each other's hands—some palms sweaty with nerves, others cold as death.

The first note from Lady White fleeted hauntingly through the air, sending pins and needles to their flesh. They sang along, trance-like, a chorus of shaky baritones and meek sopranos. When the last note faded, an eerie silence and heavy stillness pervaded.

Their nervous eyes looked at one another before fixing on Lady White. Her head was slightly bowed. Through closed lids, her eyes darted back and forth, back and forth, like a sleeper amidst a dream—or nightmare.

The scent of lavender suddenly permeated the room. One guest, a Mr. Baxton, looked about, sure that someone had spritzed perfume. It was his first time attending a séance, and he questioned Lady White's credibility. He was certain it was all a scam but promised his mother, who sat to his right holding his hand, that he would attend. Mrs. Baxton was a frequent guest at these events and claimed that Lady White had reunited her with her husband, the late Mr. Baxton, who had passed some years before.

Now that her son, the young Mr. Baxton, faced the same tragic loss of a spouse, his lovely wife perishing from an unexplained illness, she knew he would have a great sense of peace if he could only speak to her one last time. It was all poppycock if you asked him. Yet, the scent of lavender unnerved him.

His wife loved lavender.

Beads of sweat began to drip like candle wax down his face.

The flames wavered in a mysterious breeze, and Lady White's head jerked upright. The guests jolted in unison, squeezing each other's hands.

Her lids creaked open—a milky sheen clouded her blue eyes like the first signs of a storm on a summer's day. The very room seemed charged. All the tiny hairs on their skin stood on end.

Lady White's head turned left, then crept towards the right as again she looked at each guest. *Will it be my Timothy?* one guest thought. *Oh, I do hope it is my sweet sister*, thought another. But—no. This spirit came forth for Mr. Baxton.

Lady White's eyes darted back to him. "George?" Her voice sounded deeper, less enchanting. "Is that you, George?"

Mr. Baxton's mother squeezed his hand. "It is quite alright. Talk to her," she whispered. He opened his mouth but could not muster any words.

"Oh, George," said Lady White, with the exact cadence of his late wife. "How I loved you, husband." She looked at Mr. Baxton with a sinister smile. Like insects skittling up his back to sink their poison in his neck, chills ran up his spine. *It is all a trick!* he told himself.

"Say *something* to her, George," urged his mother.

"Yes—er—it is I, George, your husband. Are you—quite at peace?"

For a moment, Lady White only looked at him. Then, tilting her head, she sprouted in laughter. A cackle as startling as thunder. Everyone shifted in their seats, never letting go of hands but looking at Mr. Baxton with uncertainty.

His cheeks twitched between a delirious smile and a terrified frown.

Finally, Lady White's laughter ceased, and the storm previously held at bay poured forth from the clouds. Her face tensed. "How dare you," she said through clenched teeth. "You despicable man!"—here, everyone gasped—"You know I am not at peace!"

Mr. Baxton paled. His whole body trembled like a frightened pup. "I'm sorry," he croaked.

"Sorry? That is all you have to say for yourself?" Lady White's eyes grew so wide they looked about to pop out of their sockets and roll onto the table. Mr. Baxton couldn't take it. Ready to flee, he released the hands holding onto his. Without warning, Lady White clambered over the table. She toppled onto Mr. Baxton, sending them flying backward in his chair.

Screams and shouts filled the room, but no one screamed as loud as Mr. Baxton. Lady White, or rather, the enraged spirit of his dear wife, clawed at his eyes like a feral wolf.

A subtle tap-tap-tap to the door awakened Dr. Seward. He sat up with a snort, the clock ticking on the mantle loud and jarring. Rank pools of sweat dampened his underarms, the musty scent lingering and stagnant in his office. He raked his hands over his receding hairline, rubbed his eyes. Morning light, golden and bright, leaked through the closed curtains. He released a heavy sigh. He fell asleep at his desk. His wife would not be pleased. She had expected him home for dinner.

The knock came again. He cleared his throat and stood, unsteady. "Yes, do come in."

His assistant, a recent graduate from Oxford, Doctor Gregory Taylor peeked in, round spectacles glistening. He appeared fresh and ready for the day: brown hair swept neatly back, fashionable waistcoat and jacket creased and crisp. "Excuse me, Doctor, but it is nine o'clock and, your wife sent a message." His alert gaze drifted to the empty bottle of whiskey on Dr. Seward's desk.

"Right. Thank you, Gregory." He plopped back into his leather chair, weary. "Please have Mrs. Hawthorne bring tea."

Gregory nodded but did not leave.

"Is there more, Gregory?" Dr. Seward rubbed at his temples, annoyed.

"Yes, Doctor. We received word that a new patient is arriving today. A Lady Victoria White." Gregory walked in and laid a thin envelope upon the desk. "Her file—it is quite...unique."

"Pray, tell me more." The doctor leaned back in his chair, ignoring the envelope and wishing for tea.

Gregory stood by the large cedar desk, wringing his hands and shuffling his feet. Being around Dr. Seward in this state always made him uneasy. "She is a woman of high class, Doctor. But she claims to be a medium and is known for holding séances frequently at her estate. Has quite the following, in fact. However, at the last supposed séance, things didn't go so well."

"Yes, do go on."

"Well, in attendance was Mr. Baxton, a recent widower. Lady White presumably summoned her spirit, and in doing so, attacked Mr. Baxton."

"How so?" asked Dr. Seward, interest piqued.

"She gouged his eyes out, Doctor. With her fingernails." Gregory raised his brows. "The man is blind."

Dr. Seward sat up. "And what was her reasoning?"

"She claims that Mr. Baxton murdered his wife and the spirit came forth, seeking revenge."

"I see," Dr. Seward sighed.

"But that is not all."

"Oh?"

"It seems that Lady White is a recent widow herself. Her husband, Lord White, died last spring by a fall from the stairs. He was much older than her, this being his second marriage, and everyone agreed in his weakened state, tripped and fell to his death. They have no heirs, so naturally, his fortune went to his wife. But after this recent event, the authorities question if his fall was, in fact, an accident."

Dr. Seward's mind reeled. He had seen this before: A woman treated poorly by men all her life. Most put up with it while others…snap. He couldn't blame them. Why, he even had several patients brought to him for simply disobeying their husbands. However, not many cases led to violence…or death.

"When does she arrive, Gregory?"

"Within the hour, Doctor."

"Right. Please have tea and toast brought in. Alert me as soon as the patient arrives."

When Gregory shut the door, Dr. Seward scrambled to hide the remnants of his drink and the bottle of chloral (that he prayed went unnoticed by the prying eyes of his protégé).

He then opened a drawer in his desk and pulled out a change of clothes. It wasn't the first time he had spent the night in his office, nor would it be the last. When he married Marjorie, a beautiful and brilliant woman with dark hair and large hazel eyes, he promised himself he would never take another drug again. And he kept to his promise for many months. But as time went on, the painful memories of the past resurfaced like the dead who walked amongst the living. Flashing images staked his brain: splattered blood, crucifixes held in trembling hands, gleaming fangs, decapitated heads, rolling and rolling. One head in particular.

A head with golden hair and porcelain skin.

He became skittish and unreliable. The smallest sound in the night caused him to panic and seize a weapon, sure that the Count had returned, this time to take Marjorie as his bride. So, to ease this madness, he began taking tiny portions of opium, then chloral, sometimes mixing the two with his after-supper drink. He poured himself into his work as the drugs poured into him, and became a prized doctor—albeit slightly crazed—and well-known for treating and diagnosing diseases of the mind yet, with a disease of his own.

A disease of guilt.

He could never forgive himself for what they did to Lucy.

Dr. Seward was changing behind a dressing screen when Mrs. Hawthorne—a woman in her late years with graying hair and kind, wrinkled eyes, whose presence brought a mother-like comfort to Dr. Seward—entered with a rattling tray. "Your tea, Doctor," she said. "I'll bring in a wash bin shortly." Unbeknownst to him, the staff was well acquainted with his habits but said nothing of them. He paid their wages and offered job security, which in turn kept their lips sealed. Besides, the Doctor did fine work.

"Thank you, Mrs. Hawthorne. Whatever would I do without you," he said from behind the screen. After two cups of tea, a pile of toast, fresh clothes, a shave (and a sneaky sip of whiskey), Dr. Seward received word that his new patient had arrived, and he set off to meet her.

The keys clattered, and the door unlocked with an echoing click.

Lady White sat on the edge of a thin cot, her back to the door. She wore a dull cotton smock the color of straw, and her hair—lucky to have missed the scissors upon arrival—looked girlish in a plain plait atop her head. Her swan-like neck, a neck the

Count would have loved to sink his teeth into, looked vulnerable and bare.

Dr. Seward entered with Gregory at his heels. The room smelt of flowers on a spring day—quite different from the cell's usual scent of dampness—and the slits of the sun passing between the bars of the small square window provided surprising warmth.

Dr. Seward paused a few feet away from his patient. "Lady White?"

She turned her head to the side; the shackles bounding her hands and feet clinked like bells. The sun illuminated her fair hair and skin then, shining like a halo about her head.

Dr. Seward's eyes softened, and his mouth formed a subtle smile. *An angel come to save me from this life full of evil and dread,* he thought. But then, he took in her bright blue eyes and blonde, golden hair. *Lucy?* His heart stopped beating. *Is it my Lucy?*

"Hello, Doctor," she said.

Dr. Seward blinked. Closed his mouth. Her voice…it was… *different.* Why was her voice different? He took a deep breath, and Gregory, from behind, shuffled his feet.

"Are you quite alright, Doctor?" Lady White asked, her round blue eyes concerned. "You look to have seen a ghost."

A ghost. That was, in fact, what Dr. Seward thought to be staring at. After a long moment, he released a nervous laugh. "You remind me of someone." This was not how he first greeted a patient. He should never disclose that information. But oh, how she looked so much like Lucy.

He walked over to her and sat on the opposite side of the cot, hands shaking. She turned to fully face him, while Gregory stood in a corner to observe, notebook open and ready.

"I am Dr. Seward," he told her, gaining back control of his nerves.

"Yes, so I am told," she said with a pout to her lips.

He stifled a gasp. Lucy had had the same look when she didn't get her way. He *loved* that look. He flicked his eyes to the floor; a tiny black spider crawled along a crevice, bringing forth a memory of Renfield. *What is going on?* He thought. *Too many memories.*

"I can assure you, Doctor. I am *not* mad." Her voice was a lullaby amidst the howling of his thoughts.

He lifted his gaze and their eyes locked. She waited for him to respond. A long moment passed in silence. *What is happening?* Dr. Seward thought again. *It is as if Lucy is reincarnated and sitting before me now.* Finally, Gregory stepped forward, questioning the doctor with his furrowed brows. "It is for us to determine, Lady White. You may not think you are mad, but something caused you to attack Mr. Baxton."

"I have repeated my story several times," she retorted. "It was his wife's spirit who took control. I did not know what I was doing until she had left my body. I woke up to blood on my hands and the authorities taking me away!" Her bottom lip trembled.

"Do calm yourself, Lady White," Gregory said.

Dr. Seward, coming to his senses, put up one hand. "Gregory, can you please give us a moment?"

Gregory cocked his head in indignation. The doctor had never asked him to leave. "Are you certain?" He looked from Dr. Seward to Lady White, then back to the doctor, implying it was not safe for him to be alone.

"Yes, Gregory. I will be fine. I can call a guard if needed."

"As you wish." Gregory walked out the door, head hanging.

Dr. Seward waited till the sound of his boots faded down the desolate hall before he turned back to his patient. "I apologize, Lady White—"

"Please, call me Victoria."

"Victoria...let us start from the beginning. Shall we?"

She lowered her chin, long eyelashes raised.

"Right, you say the spirit took hold of your body. How does this phenomenon occur?"

"Well," she said, turning her head to the side as if recalling a dream, "at first, the spirit speaks to my mind, tells me who they are and why they have come." She spoke kindly now, as if having a conversation over tea and not in a cell. "If I feel they have come for good reasons, I let them in."

"What do you mean, let them in?" asked Dr. Seward, resisting the urge to scoot in closer. "It is hard to explain, Doctor. It is like the top of my skull cracks open, and the clouds of spirits swirling above swarm down into my brain, but…only one makes it through. The one I choose to let in."

Dr. Seward thought about this, and after a pause, asked: "And why did you choose to let in Mrs. Baxton?"

Her expression grew sorrowful. Eyes tearful. She clasped her hands, rattling the cuffs. "Because Doctor, her husband, Mr. Baxton…murdered her."

"I see," he replied. "How did this murder occur?"

"I—don't know. She only told me he killed her. And she must seek revenge."

Dr. Seward harrumphed.

"I know it's hard to believe, Doctor. But I guarantee if her body were exhumed and examined, they would find something sinister afoot. She *did not* perish from a simple illness."

"I believe *you* believe this to be true, Victoria. However, I will put in a word with the authorities and see what we can discover."

Pleased, her heart-shaped lips lifted in a sweet yet sad smile that made the doctor's heart ache. "And once this spirit comes through, do you lose all sense of control?" he asked, knowing he was losing *his* sense of control in her presence.

"Yes, Doctor. When the spirit enters, everything goes black. It is as if I am dead myself. My soul is replaced by theirs."

"I see." Sweat licked at his palms. "Did this happen when your husband fell?"

Her body tensed. In a whispery, dread-filled tone, she asked: "Why do you ask such a question?"

"He was married before, yes? Did his first wife's spirit enter your vessel and push him down the stairs?"

She was silent, staring, and sad, and he knew then that her husband had not fallen on accident. The quiver to her lips told him so. "We shall come back to that." He got up from the cot with a creak. "I'll let you rest now, Victoria. I'll visit you tomorrow morning." He turned to leave, reluctant to depart from her.

"Doctor?"

He spun back around. "Yes?"

Her eyes swarmed around the invisible space about him. The previous warmth of the room faded. An icy chill crept in, and their breath formed like a shroud around their faces.

"There is a shadow that follows you closely. A black shadow. So close it looks almost like your own. It is sad for you, Doctor. So sad and...so angry." She looked up at him, her pale face shocked by this new knowledge she spun from the air.

"Tomorrow, Lady White," he croaked. "We shall continue tomorrow." He left before she could say anything further; but he felt her eyes on his back long after the thick, heavy door locked behind him. They followed him like a black shadow.

T hat night, Dr. Seward did not go home for dinner. After his rounds, he spent hours pacing back and forth in his office, recording his interview with Lady White into his phonograph and speculating on her prognosis. What he failed to record, and what really inhabited his mind, was he *believed* in Lady White. He did not want to. He wanted more than anything to prove her mad—as everyone expected of him. But his studies under Van Helsing taught him to not overlook the supernatural. *There lies more to the mind than what is seen and studied.* How could he dismiss anything out of the ordinary after facing an evil that defied all odds? Also, it could be no coincidence that Victoria looked so much like Lucy. But was it her resemblance that was clouding his judgment? He knew she was a murderess—possessed or not. Should he turn to his usual, tried and true procedures? He couldn't bear to see her beautiful limbs crisscrossed in a strait jacket, or water spewing from her mouth from a cold plunge, blundering and gasping for breath. No—he must approach this case in a different manner.

He filled a glass with two fingers full of whiskey. Bringing it to his lips, consumed by the luring scent of alcohol, it came to him. He knew what must be done. With the liquid undulating like oceans of time, so did Lady White's words: *There is a shadow that follows you closely. A black shadow. So close it looks almost like your own. It is sad for you, Doctor. So sad and...so angry.*

He tipped back the glass and drank her wave of words away.

C andle flames wavered like spindly fingers. Long, hand-like shadows writhed and danced across the leather-bound books and paintings as if searching for a victim to grab and claim. The smell of candlewax permeated Dr. Sewards's office, commingling with the soured scent of his nerves.

Lady White sat across from him on a small table covered by a white cloth. The nearby lamps, swathed in red silk, smothered her pale skin in fresh, blood-filled light. Dr. Seward's heart skipped beat after beat. At this moment, he wished he had listened to Gregory. *It is unconventional and dangerous, Doctor!* Gregory had said.

Disgruntled, Dr. Seward had shouted, *Have my plans not worked before, Gregory? There is much you do not know of. You have barely touched the surface of what ripples in the mind.* He felt bad for yelling, and even debated telling Gregory everything then... but decided against it. Best to let the chap be innocent of the unknown. Why poison his young mind too?

In the end, Gregory agreed to help. He went to Lady White and soon returned, confirming she obliged to hold a séance and had given him a list of items and requirements she needed to do so. Mrs. Hawthorne prepared Dr. Seward's office without question, and when a billowy blanket of stars filled the sky, and the bellied moon woke from its slumber, they brought Lady White in, ghostly and vampiric with her pale skin and matching smock.

Now that they sat facing one another, he wasn't so sure of this idea. A harrowing knot of worry twisted in his chest. This didn't *feel* right. Even knowing Gregory and a guard were waiting outside did nothing to reassure him.

She reached across the table, palms open, beckoning to be held. He looked down, eyeing her delicate wrist, her long fingers, so like the shadows scratching about the walls.

I should have called for Professor Van. Helsing, he thought. *He would know what to do but—* Seeking help would also bring forth his habits. Van Helsing would see through his secrets. Arthur and

Jonathan would be no help. They all avoided each other like a sickness. Their presence only brought forth the horrible remembrances burrowed deep within their souls, rotting not only this life but also their next. Cursed for eternity. *Is that not what the Count felt? Cursed for eternity?*

"We must hold hands, Doctor," Lady White said, knowing he was lost in the clinging cobwebs of his mind.

Dr. Seward gave a shake of his head and straightened his back. "Of course." He clasped her hands in his. A thrill of energy charged through his bones. Chills scoured his flesh.

Lady White inhaled. "No matter what happens, Doctor, remember to keep hold of my hands." She tightened her grip. "Never let go."

He swallowed in silent agreement.

"We will begin with a hymn." Lady White closed her eyes and, after a moment—a moment that felt like his cursed eternity—she began to sing. Instantly, Dr. Seward was lost again, not in his thoughts, but in Lady White's haunting song. The room filled with the melancholy voice of an angel mourning a soul it could never save. Dr. Seward's heavy heart pulsed and pulsed in rhythm with her words. He fought back tears, his throat choked with sorrow. For the hymn—one he had never heard before—sounded more like a dirge.

When her singing came to an end, he exhaled with relief, not knowing more sorrow was soon to come.

Lady White bowed her head.

Time stood still.

She sat as stiff as the undead awaiting the night. The shadows about the room danced no more; the burning candles and wax slipping and sliding petrified right before his eyes. "Victoria?" She did not answer. Instead, a steady *tick-tick-tick* sounded on the barred windows (for even in a doctor's office, there was no escape). Dr. Seward shook. *A bat!—trying to get in!* Horrified, he turned his attention to the window, clotted by curtains. *Tick-tick-tick.* The sound came again. All at once, a splatter smacked the hidden pane and rattled the glass. He jolted, almost releasing Lady White's hand. A rumble reverberated then, and Dr. Seward realized it was rain he heard. A storm. *The undead...can control the elements*, his webby mind thought.

Delirious, he turned back to Lady White and froze.

Above her head a warm light swarmed about. Like fairy dust, it sparked and shimmered and, for a moment, hope glided into Dr. Seward's chest. Soon after, another substance formed: an obsidian mass that sucked the brightness into its depths. It grew larger and darker—looming above Lady White in a mountain of blackness. Black as the blood of Dracula's heart. And with this shadow, a pungent scent seized Dr. Seward's senses. Sweet and sharp and unmistakable. *The scent of garlic blooms.*

The blackness twirled above Lady White's bowed head and, much to Dr. Seward's dismay, poured right into the top of her skull. Her head snapped up like a puppet come to life, and Dr. Seward shot back in his seat.

She tightened her small hands around his, nails digging into this skin—the same nails that clawed the eyes of Mr. Baxton weeks before. Dr. Seward almost called for help, so sure Lady White was about to attack, when her malice evaporated like smoke. Her grip loosened, countenance softened, and like a pleased lover, her face melted into one of titillating beauty.

"John? Oh, John," she cooed, eyelids fluttering like bat wings. "My doctor. My dear, doctor." Her voice was sweet as syrup. "How I have missed you, Jack."

Jack? he thought. *No one knows me by that name except—*

"Lucy?" he spluttered, eyes wide and heart bouncing.

"Why, of course, Jack. Who else could it be? Do you have another love, Jack? You naughty boy!" she giggled. The edge of Dr. Seward's lips lifted.

Then, as quick as the change of the tide, the tide that ushered in the Count's ship, her mood shifted again. She brought her chin towards her chest, eyes raised. "I am disappointed in you," she pouted. "I know *all* your secrets. I have watched you fade into oblivion—too many times, my dear Doctor."

He frowned. "I—can't cope with...what we did to you," he cried, eyes rimmed with tears. "It haunts me day and night, Lucy." His hands trembled in hers. "I will never forgive myself."

"You *let* him do it, John," she spat. "You *let* Arthur put a stake through my heart. I thought you loved me, Jack."

"I do love you!"

"You chopped off my head! How could you do that to someone you love?"

Dr. Seward sobbed like a baby.

"Shh, Jack," she whispered with a bashful smile. "I know how we can make things right."

"How?" He asked, snot dripping from his nose.

"Do you trust me? She ran her thumbs over the top of his hand. "You *must* trust me."

"Of course, Lucy. Of course, I trust you."

"I thought so, Jack. I should have chosen you instead of Arthur. He has long moved on. But you, my sweet Doctor, mourn my loss every day. Now, we shall be together."

A crack of thunder bellowed with her words. The sounds of disturbed patients in their cells, banging and moaning reverberated through the asylum and into his office as the rain pattered on the roof.

"What do you mean?" Dr. Seward whispered.

Lucy's lips spread wide into a teasing smile. So wide, he glimpsed the edge of fangs, glimmering as if already stained with blood.

"One bite and we shall be together."

Dr. Seward pulled his hands away, repulsed.

Eyes red as flames, Lucy snarled and jumped across the table, landing atop her prey within the blink of an eye. Dr. Seward squirmed and squealed, writhed and wailed. It was no use. Her fangs met his neck. As pinpricks of pain and pleasure punctured into his soft, sweaty skin, pulling pools of blood from his veins, Dr. Seward, finally succumbed. For a moment, complete and utter bliss consumed and cleared his mind. All his worries, all his guilt, gone with her kiss.

The dark kiss of his dear Lucy.

"Doctor!" Gregory yelled. Hearing the commotion, he barged through the door and grabbed hold of Lady White, breaking the blood bond. Wild-eyed, she screamed for her doctor, a thin river of blood running down her delicate chin. Gregory passed her to the guards, shocked by her inhuman strength and befuddled by her sharp, yapping teeth.

Dr. Seward lay whimpering on the floor, one hand on the bleeding wound on his neck, the other outstretched. Gregory hurried over to him. "I am here, Doctor. You will be just fine. It appears to be a minor injury."

"No!" Dr. Seward wailed. "You don't understand. Bring her back to me." He grabbed Gregory's collar with a bloody hand, a manic glint in his eyes, and whispered: "*My* Lucy has returned."

Jasmine De La Paz is a Gothic horror author based in Bishop, CA. With lush landscapes, historical settings, and sinister characters, her stories explore the strange, the macabre, and the beauty within the darkness. Many anthologies and literary magazines feature her work, including Love Letters To Poe Vol. 3, Tenebrous Antiquities, Quill & Crow Publishing, Thin Veil Press, Dark Winter Lit, and more. You can find Jasmine online at:

www.jasminedelapaz.com

Painting Phantoms
By Doris V. Sutherland

Dr. Seward's Diary

10 March.—At long last, we discharged Perry, the gentleman who believed the other patients to be somehow possessing him in the manner of evil spirits. His tendency towards violence in retaliating against this perceived menace prompted us to seclude him periodically. Even our chloral hydrate sedative was of little use. Yet his time doing productive work in the asylum grounds (he had been an accomplished gardener prior to joining us, I gather) seems to have helped in stabilising his mental state, and today, we pronounced him recovered.

If I could only make the same pronouncement in regard to myself. But I cannot. Not after having seen her again last night.

I dreamt of Lucy rising from her tomb. The visions of her wasting away on her deathbed, as heartrending as they may be, are an order of magnitude easier to bear than those in which she is a member of (as my old mentor would say) the Un-dead. The most appalling aspect of these latter nightmares is their way of investing me with terrible *knowledge*. Dreams are often like this, allowing us to grasp the workings of their illogical landscapes; and in these Lucy-dreams, I know what is occupying her un-dead mind. I understand her appetites. I feel her devotion to her accursed groom. I am aware of how nothing at all of sweet Lucy Westenra remains in that cold, pale head.

Such thoughts I must bear as I tend to my patients. *Quis custodiet ipsos custodes?* Indeed!

Edna Seward's Diary

10 March.—Jack awoke in the night again. He woke me up too, clambering about in such haste that he got tangled in our bedclothes and fell to the floor. We're lucky that he escaped injury. His yelling was frightful, even before he hit his jaw on the cabinet. I find myself struggling to sleep too, given how I'm always expecting another of his fearful turns. It was an occasional disorder when we first married. Now it's a matter of nightly dread.

He's able to treat his patients with almost the same degree of energy and sympathy as before, but I wonder how long this'll last. The rest of the day was uneventful.

Letter from Dr. Seward to Havelock Ellis.

11 March.

Dear Havelock Ellis,

I am unsure if you remember me. We met when I was among the gentlemen in the Free Press Defence Committee that banded together during that absurd legal tussle over your book on sexual inversion. I was not one of the more prominent members, but I remain proud to have played my role in breaking superannuated taboos. Turning a blind eye to matters that we deem foolish or improper does not eliminate our problems; it merely allows evil to fester. I have seen this with my own eyes.

I write to you because I understand that you are working on a volume about the mechanics of dreams. I have recently been troubled by nightmares and would very much like to volunteer as a research subject for your project. (My purposes are not entirely unselfish: if anyone might cure my disorder, it is surely yourself.)

With admiration,
Dr. John Seward

Letter from Havelock Ellis to Dr. Seward.

18 March.

My dear Dr. Seward,

Of course I remember you! And be assured that your contributions to the campaign against my book's suppression were no less valuable than those of Shaw, Harris or Hyndman. I also recall how, when meeting your charming wife and yourself, we touched upon some of your work at the sanitarium. I always felt that I had seen only the uppermost layer of your experience. I would certainly appreciate the opportunity to speak further; and with your permission, I would be willing to arrange another meeting in person.

With regards,
Havelock Ellis

Edna Seward's Diary

25 March.—Jack's recent change in mood has done much to set my heart at ease. At long last, we can discuss his patients without him bringing up his own ailments. We've even returned to our happy conversations about the future of our family. When I suggested giving our daughter (our still hypothetical daughter!) the name Ira in honour of my favourite aunt, Jack granted full approval. The first time that we've agreed on such matters!

The reason for this atmosphere of hope is that my beloved doctor has found a physician of his own, one who'll be visiting in due course. A little regrettably, it's Havelock Ellis.

I recall Mr. Ellis from that meeting when he mistook me for a housekeeper. After Jack had introduced me properly and cleared the error, Ellis remarked on how he'd occasionally encountered black men married to white women, but he'd never before seen the opposite arrangement. Since then, I've held some idea of how zoo animals feel when stared at by fascinated children. But while I can't honestly look forward to having that man in our home again, I still hold hope that Jack's distemper shall at last be cured.

Havelock Ellis' Diary

10 April.—Arrived in Purfleet to meet my correspondent Dr. John Seward. We discussed his recurring dream regarding a young woman of gaunt, cadaverous aspect. His nightmare reminded me of a commonplace motif that I have identified in dreams and myths alike: that of the ghostly lover. The story of Orpheus and Euridice comes immediately to mind; I also recall that Lafcadio Hearn, in his writings on Japan, outlined a dream told to him by a local in which the pale likeness of a deceased lady appeared beside her grave.

As we discussed these matters in his drawing room, Seward seemed uncomfortable, on account (I rather suspect) of the archetypal virgin being associated in his dream with disease and death. I tried to explain to him that our subconscious minds frequently take symbols of innocence and distort them in ways that might strike us as bizarre, unnatural, or even monstrous.

"I can recall dreaming," I said to him, "of children with large flowers instead of heads, their eyes staring from among the petals. Another time I dreamt of an albatross transforming into a woman whose nose still resembled a beak. And then there was my dream of an artificial woman."

Seward appeared intrigued and asked me to elaborate. The conversation was beginning to seem somewhat frivolous—I was not, after all, here to discuss my dreams—but I reminded myself that it was merely vulgar prejudice that confined dreams to the realms of the childish. There was no harm in the two of us exchanging our nighttime visions.

"Yes, she was a sort of doll," I explained, "one that would have taken a master craftsman to design. Parts of her were more convincing than others. The skin of her breasts, the hair of her armpits, seemed so real as to be horrifying. But her left arm recalled a child's ill-made toy. Yet she could walk, could even talk, giving answers to questions. It does rather make you wonder if the Pygmalion narrative arose from just such a dream."

It transpired that I was right to pursue this line of conversation, as Seward became more relaxed and candid in describing his nightmares.

"Sometimes," he told me, "I see the woman rising from her tomb. In other instances, she enters my room through the closed door."

"By breaking it?"

"No. Rather, by shrinking herself to fit through the merest crack. She will then approach me, baring those accursed teeth."

"Teeth?"

"Why, yes, she has elongated canines. Fangs. You see, Lucy drinks blood, and usually wears a white garment stained in red…"

I interrupted him. "Lucy?"

At that moment, Dr. Seward slipped back into his prior discomfort. He exchanged glances with his wife, whose expression was as inscrutable as always. Then he spoke up.

"Yes, well, I give the ghost-girl a nickname, I suppose you could say. Lucy."

"Is there significance to this name?"

"I fear that I may have picked up a habit or two from my patients," said Seward. "We have a gentleman who lives in fear of a man named Ned who supposedly arrives at night, and a girl who is convinced that a family of three named Mary, Stephen and Fanny live under the floorboards."

Our conversation entered a digression about people's habit of applying nicknames to supposed ghosts. Seward brought up the celebrated haunting of Willington Mill, whose purported spectre was dubbed Old Jeffrey. Mrs. Seward provided a few accounts from her own colourful upbringing. But the purpose of our meeting was to discuss dreams, and so dreams we resumed discussing.

"I would like to know," I said to Seward, "about the precise emotions that you feel when experiencing these dreams."

His response to this question was awkward and evasive, as was to be expected. Given his profession, he was unaccustomed to describing anything that might be taken as a disorder of his own mind. He identified only physical sensations—the coldness of the night air, the dampness of the crypt—and not the emotions about which I had specifically asked him. It was only after considerable (if gentle) encouragement from Mrs. Seward that he admitted to sometimes awakening, in rapt terror, with the conviction that Lucy was in the room with him and that he must escape as soon as possible.

Here, I must have exclaimed with triumph, as I recognised the pattern into which Dr. Seward's dreams were fitting.

"And during these encounters, do you have an accelerated heartbeat and faster respiration?"

He replied in the affirmative, saying that it took his wife's care to calm him down and reassure him of his safety.

At last, we had a potential cause.

"When we sleep with a stomach that is disturbed or perhaps distended," I explained, "this can lead to an excitement of our hearts and lungs which, in turn, may produce an intense emotional agitation. Our sleeping consciousness is forced to produce an explanation for our physical disorders, and we awake with some false notion in our heads. This might be a belief that there is a present threat, in other cases, an intense guilt over a crime that, in reality, we have not committed. In your case, you believe Lucy to be in your house."

I described to him similar cases that I have encountered in my research. A farmer's daughter dreamed of seeing her deceased brother with bloody fingers; upon awakening, she tried to comfort herself with the knowledge that it was merely a dream, only to feel a hand gripping her shoulder. This turned out to be merely an involuntary muscular twitch.

Of course, that young lady had been dreaming of a lost loved one. How, then, to account for this figure of Lucy who had intruded herself upon Seward's sleep? The details of fangs and blood-drinking struck me as reminiscent of certain folktales from Eastern Europe and the Levant regarding vampires, which gave me an idea for my next question.

"What do you prefer to read before retiring to bed, Dr. Seward?"

He seemed perplexed. "Why do you ask?"

"Well," I replied. "I am merely thinking of a personal incident. You see, I had been reading a work by Wilhelm Joest, the German ethnographer, describing his time in Africa. At one point he had been sketching a young lady because he was interested in her tribal tattoos. After a while she grew bored and—" (here, I confess, I became somewhat embarrassed, but continued with the narrative in the interests of science) "—squeezed her breasts together, causing milk to spray into Joest's face. She then ran away in a state of laughter. That image lingered in my mind and informed my dreams the following night. I saw a woman who had a penis between her legs, and she was using it to spray fluids just as I had pictured that African spraying milk."

Dr. Seward stared, and Mrs. Seward appeared quite flustered. I realise that, *mea culpa*, I had strayed into excessive detail about a somewhat inappropriate area of my studies. I decided to return the conversation to its essential topic.

"So, I merely wondered if you tend to read upon subjects that might likewise inform your dreams. Stories regarding vampires, for example."

I noticed here a shadow falling over Seward's face. Even after I had stopped talking, he showed no inclination to offer his own thoughts; he merely stared at me, or rather *through* me. I realised to what extent my anecdote might have touched upon uncomfortable matters. It now seemed apt to change the subject, bringing up something that I had long hoped to mention: medication.

"Have you ever read Thomas De Quincey's *Confessions of an English Opium Eater*?" I asked Seward, who shook his head in response. "He saw the visual phenomena conjured by opium and other such drugs as a revival of a faculty possessed naturally by children. He referred to it as the practice of painting phantoms upon the darkness, I believe. As a boy, Dr. Seward, did you never close your eyes tight and see marvellous visions?"

"Yes," he said. "It was akin to looking through a kaleidoscope."

"I recall an incident from when I was around seven," I continued. "I was with a certain cousin of the same age, and we buried our heads in our pillows to see wondrous successions of images. The fascinating detail is that the two of us shared the same visions. When I saw the images change from one thing to another, my cousin would call out at that precise moment that he had seen the same change."

Seward appeared intrigued by this notion, and asked various questions which, alas, I was unable to answer. As I had to inform him, the simple truth was that the psychologists of childhood have long neglected this phenomenon. Those tantalising, unanswered questions hung over much of our following conversation, which lasted for too long for me to transcribe; suffice to say that it turned to wish-dreams, erotic symbols and the like. Mrs. Seward appeared to be suppressing fits of mirth, and so I decided to move on to the matter of how Dr. Seward should respond to his ailment.

Although I was unable to prescribe a cure, as such, I informed him of my recent research into drugs. Before our meeting ended, I provided mescal buttons and directions on their usage. I await his report as to their effects.

Edna Seward's Diary

10 April.—Havelock Ellis came and went. He was more agreeable than on his previous visit, but I've never before heard a man go on about his dreams at such enormous length. It was like hearing a tiny tot gush about the contents of Grimm's Fairy Tales or the *Arabian Nights*—except that, to the best of my recollection, none of those stories included visions of women with male organs.

I'm still tittering at one particular part of Ellis' impromptu lecture:

"I spoke to a young lady who dreamed of having married her music-master and borne him a child. This dream-child was confused as to whether he was a boy or a girl, so she told him that as a musical genius, he was both in one. Another part of the dream concerned the lady's deathly fear of being beheaded; yet upon her marriage, she came to accept an impending death by strangulation, a clear symbol of the erotic wish."

Poor Jack was completely bewildered! Ellis had to explain to him that (if I recall correctly) the woman's death in her dream was meant to symbolise marriage, and her coming to accept death was a symbol of her coming to accept matrimony. If this makes sense in his mind, then I can only pity poor Mrs. Ellis, whoever she may be.

"Do you imply," Jack asked our guest, "that the girl in my dreams represents somebody for whom I am wishing?"

I was trying my best not to giggle like a schoolgirl, and Ellis launched into another lecture:

"No, not all dreams are based upon suppressed wishes. I have dreamt of being a mayor involved with the local Bible Society; a soldier in battle; even a music hall comedian. None of these are wishes of mine, although I suppose that they might be termed vestigial possibilities: echoes of directions that my life may once have taken. I have even dreamt that I had died and was in the process of undergoing autopsy."

I couldn't help interrupting at this point to remark on how alarming it must have been to find oneself in such a position.

"Well, I did not exactly find myself on the table," Ellis admitted, "as I was not quite myself in the dream, if you understand my meaning. I had been replaced with an ugly old woman."

Most of the conversation went along similarly nonsensical lines before Ellis eventually prescribed (of all things!) the buttons of a certain cactus which I believe is known to the Spaniards as peyote. I'll admit that I didn't voice my apprehensions.

Dr. Seward's Diary

10 April.—The meeting with Havelock Ellis was fascinating, if a trifle exhausting. My inability to tell him the truth about poor Lucy's ordeal weighed heavily upon me. We discussed the possible influence of dreams upon myths, which made me recall a line from Hobbes' *Leviathan* regarding the ignorance of how to distinguish dreams from reality which prompted the Gentiles to worship satyrs, fawns and nymphs, and in Hobbes' own time, bred belief in fairies, ghosts, goblins and witches.

In the case of Lucy, it is quite the reverse. A nymph—or rather, a siren—escaped from fable first to enter reality, and subsequently into my dreams.

Towards the end of our meeting, Ellis used a phrase that has lingered in my mind. He spoke of how our dreams allow us to see into "the Utgard of the subconscious." I grasp the analogy well enough. In Norse myth, Utgard was the home of the giants, the dread foes of Odin; not the oafish giants of the nursery or story-book, but shapeshifting, intangible beings of nightmare. I understand that there were Utgard-maidens as well as Utgard-men.

Ellis provided a sample of mescal, a drug with which the Indians visit their own Utgards. Could this truly provide a means of vanquishing my accursed dreams? Only time will tell. For now, I have a duty to my patients. I shall try Mr. Ellis' remedy either when time permits, or when Lucy's visitations become sufficiently grave to allow no other recourse.

Dr. Seward's Diary

12 April.—The brief reprieve is over. Lucy came last night. I saw her in the room again: there was not even the small mercy of the transportation to another land that sometimes comes with dreams. Not only that, I felt her touch. Her hands, her — no. I must write no more. I must attempt Mr. Ellis' unorthodox medication, and so this is to be a journal of science.

What follows is a description of my experiences with mescal, which I intend to write as my experiment proceeds. As per Ellis' instructions, I have made a decoction from three mescal buttons which I shall imbibe over the course of two hours, drinking small portions at regular intervals.

1 p.m.—My first dose.

1:20 p.m.—My second dose. So far, no effect.

1:40 p.m.—By my third dose, I have begun to feel conscious of energy spreading through my body and a growth in my physical capacity. I feel as though I might run two miles or lift furniture.

2:00 p.m.—I took my fourth dose. The positive effects are abating, replaced with new, more disturbing symptoms. My pulse is low and my head faint. I recall Ellis informing me of this unsteadiness as a common effect of the mescal. As I write these words, I find that the colours of objects around my study have become enhanced, as in a gaudy painting. When I close my eyes I see vivid afterimages. Plain or blank objects, such as the paper on which I am presently writing, play host to distorted shadows. My faintness persists and I am resisting the temptation to retire to my bed.

2:12 p.m.—I return to report a development in my symptoms. Ellis described seeing vivid, jewel-like shades, but I see colours from a very different palette. The red of dried blood. The pale yellow of moonlight. The sickly green of decay. Closing my eyes plagues me with visions which I dare not describe lest they become fixed in my consciousness.

2:16 p.m.—I feel a sensation of pushing or squeezing against my left and right sides. My sense of orientation is disrupted. Even as I sit at my desk, I feel as though I am already lying supine. I also experience odours with no discernable cause: the dank aroma of lichen-covered stone, and the stench of the charnel-house.

My eyelids grow heavy, but I cannot bear to close them for fear of seeing those forms and outlines coalescing into a figure that can only be hers. It is four minutes until my next dose, and I can only hope that it brings

2:25 p.m.—I fell asleep at my desk during the above entry. I awoke with a start. I recall my dream in detail. I was in the crypt. She was there. She approached me. I shudder at what may have happened had the chance noise of a bird striking the window not awakened me.

I lack the energy and will to rise from my chair. I can barely even write these words or keep my eyes open, yet I must, otherwise she will return, and I fear—I fear—I fear.

Edna Seward's Diary

12 April—I shall describe the day's events with as much clarity as possible.

Another incident in the night. Come morning, the house was quiet until Jack began crying. I tried to placate him but to no avail. At around one in the afternoon, Jack retired to his study and asked not to be disturbed. I occupied myself with reading, but couldn't concentrate.

About an hour and a half later, I heard a moan of despair from Jack's study followed by a heavy thud and clatter of wood. Despite his wishes, I knocked on the door. He didn't answer.

I entered and found him lying on the floor, quite unconscious. His chair had tipped over backwards. On his desk was a glass of liquid, and I recalled Mr. Ellis' instructions on making some sort of medicine from the cactus buttons. I understood what had befallen my dear Jack.

As I write, with my body and soul shaken but my mind clear, I see that the logical course of action would have been to fetch help. I confess, however, that logic had deserted me. I was overwhelmed by a compulsion, as irrational as it might be, to join my husband and retrieve him from his present state. And so (how absurd the notion now strikes me) I took the glass and drank the remaining contents.

I stood and waited for the effects to come, and come they did.

I glanced at the fireplace. It was unlit, its coals lying colourless and cold, yet as I looked I saw a brilliant blue glimmering like hot embers. These burst into flames, blue as the Brighton sea, dancing and flickering less like ordinary fire and more like the descriptions I have read of the Northern Lights. The blue flame was not the only bold colour that had appeared in the room: as I spun around, I saw how the brown leather of Jack's chair was now ruby-red, while the book-spines on the shelf glimmered emerald and topaz.

This should've been beautiful, a child's dream of Aladdin's Cave come to life. It wasn't. It was unearthly and wrong. I tried to move, but I felt palpitations begin with my heart and course through my body until I crumpled to the floor. I couldn't move, couldn't cry out, could hardly breathe. All I could do was keep my eyes closed as tight as possible.

I heard a sound in my ear, almost like singing, but from no human voice. My palms, spread on the carpet, were consumed with a burning pain. The heat spread across my body and reached my head. This was enough to jolt me, to make me lift my hands and open my eyes.

I saw glowing flames, like those of a gas lamp but in a rainbow of colours. I looked for a source and found that they emanated from my own body, yet I felt no pain. Instead, I tasted different flavours. The yellow flames reminded me of the marzipan of my girlhood, while the blue had an acid taste and the green were bitter.

There appeared a brown-red flame with a particularly noxious flavour, and I tried to rid myself of it. As I lay on the floor, still unable to right myself, I dug my fingers into my skin and tore in the hopes of finding the flame's origin. My flesh sloughed away without pain or any other sensation as though it'd been dead. I proceeded to rend and rip at my sides, then my back, then my legs until I'd finally removed my material shell as I might remove orange-peel. I was a spirit and could at last move freely once more.

Jack was still unconscious. Even in my new state I had no way of reaching him. I looked out of the study's window and all was blackness, aside from the reflection of my own face, flame-skinned, lantern-eyed. There was no help to be had beyond the walls of the building.

A new urge took over my mind. I somehow knew that, if I were to save Jack, then I would have to visit the hallway.

I exited the study (I have no recollection of opening the door; perhaps my form swept through it) and found that the hallway had taken on a new aspect, its wallpaper drained of colour to resemble dank stone, its comforting atmosphere replaced with a graveyard's air. And there, near the very end, was Lucy, exactly as I'd pictured her when hearing Jack's trembling accounts. The lank hair, the chalk-white skin, the blood trickling down her chin and staining her burial-garment. She wasn't walking; her legs were quite still; and yet she grew steadily nearer.

I wasn't her prey. My dream-self somehow knew this fact without being informed. She was heading towards Jack. But I stood between Lucy and my husband, her one obstacle.

And so I flew at her in a rage. Her face didn't change. Of course not: it was a corpse-face, blank and staring. But I knew she was angry, and inwardly, I feared her retaliation. I could see her fangs, could imagine her fingernails grown to talons after death, could imagine my unfamiliar new form being torn to pieces and scattered like a rejected love-letter

I was mere feet from her when I noticed something: a second figure by her side. A little girl, clad in a similar white garment, her dark hair lost among Lucy's weeping-willow locks. She was huddled with her face buried in that rotting garment, her arms wrapped around the woman's frame not out of a desire for protection but out of fear—fear that, were she to let go, she'd be punished. Lucy's left arm was wrapped around the girl in turn, those sharp nails digging into her back. Dabs of blood stained the child's nightdress.

Without a thought, I reached for the girl to pry her free from Lucy's grasp. When that child looked up at me, the sight of her face gave me a sudden recollection of seeing my reflection in a mirror as a girl. But no, this girl was not my younger self: her complexion was lighter than mine; and yet darker than that of Jack, with whom she also shared a certain resemblance. I then understood that, if the accursed spectre of Lucy be a figure from Jack's past, then this girl must be a figure from his future—his and mine.

Her name was Ira. This, again, was a detail inserted into my mind with the certainty that comes with a dream.

I took Ira in my arms and pulled her away from Lucy, who let out a sound like the grinding of a tomb-lid, and I sped down the hallway. I looked over my shoulder and saw the white woman deteriorating, every strand of hair, every stretch of gaunt skin, every portion of fabric dissipating and shrinking in size like soap-suds in bathwater. I felt satisfaction at watching her perish for lack of prey. At the same time, I felt the form of Ira shrinking away in my arms. This, too, satisfied me: I knew that she wasn't dying, but taking her rightful place (for the present time) as part of my own form.

I passed through the door to the study, at which point exhaustion consumed even my spirit-form, and I fell downwards to the floor.

I gather that I lost consciousness at that moment. My next memory is of Jack, now awake, shaking me by the shoulder.

Later that afternoon, I was sufficiently recovered to describe my visions to Jack. He declined to share his own experiences, offering only the following statement:

"I am Lucy's suitor no more."

I would like to thank the estate of Havelock Ellis for helping me to compile the above documents as part of my colleague Dr. Quincey Harker's wider efforts to document the full ramifications of the 1897 incident.

Ira Seward, 1939.

Just a Drop, My Darling
By Elizabeth Twist

Dr. Seward's Diary

20 June.—The women's ward attendant called on me at five o'clock this morning as the sun breached the horizon. A new patient, Miss Gilda Fortescue, was in difficulty. She was admitted for hysteria yesterday. There was nothing unusual in her case, so I had yet to meet her.

No story surprises me, here in my mad little world. After the events of seven years ago, nothing will surprise me again—that is what I would have said, before Miss Fortescue.

Her crisis came as an outburst at her place of work, a day-school for labourers' children. She threatened three little ones with decapitation, lest they suffer the pains that she suffered. Her assistant called her family. Thank God it wasn't the police. Her physician is a good man, well known to me. I agreed with him that she should come to us for rest.

His report suggested she would require laudanum and a private room, but she behaved with docility and good manners at the time of her admittance, so the warden gave her a bed in the women's dormitory. A few minutes before sunrise, she shook some fellow-patients awake, rousing them with warnings that the light was returning, and they must hide their eyes.

To avoid agitating her further, the warden put her in a locked room with a west-facing window. That particular hall has a large picture window on the east side. The just-risen sun, at its fullest power on this, the longest day of the year, painted the door of Miss Fortescue's cell a joyous orange as I arrived, as if giving her its blessing.

A curious word, *blessing*: we think of a divine gift, but originally, it meant a wound. Miss Fortescue is both.

I lose my thread. I must try to record all. She stood as I opened the door. Unafraid of the light, she seemed to glow bright gold as it struck her. Her pale hair, which she'd taken down for sleeping, stood out like a halo around her head. The white night-dress she wore, and the roses in her cheeks, made her appear an absolute angel.

She extended a dainty hand, and said "Hello," as if we were at a party. "If I understand correctly, Dr. Seward, I've misbehaved egregiously."

"You don't recall?" I asked. My notebook remained tucked in my pocket. I knew I would remember every word that fell from her mouth.

Sorrow troubled her brow. "I never do."

In that moment, I swore I would do everything I could to help her. This is a promise I make to all my patients, but in her case I meant it as a man.

My heart is at risk. I need not guess why. In her looks and her symptoms, she is Lucy Westenra. In her manner, and her soul, she is entirely herself, sweet and obliging, and full of bright intelligence.

Together we sat in her room while I took her history. She has been ill for five months now. At first she walked in her sleep, and then the emotional outbursts began. Quite logically, her doctor attributed these tantrums to a lack of rest.

I asked if she had endured any crisis that may have disturbed her mind, but she said no. Before these symptoms, her life was perfectly happy, and continued to be so despite them until more recently.

Now she suffers almost daily. Before her fits, she often has a throbbing pain in her head, or what she calls a shadow at the edge of her vision. She has used this fact to hide the severity of her illness, often making some excuse to leave the company of others before she loses herself completely.

I fear an organic cause, some disorder of the brain itself, but no: I should not think it. Many lunatics have had some difficulty or trial they don't remember consciously. Even the most disturbed people skew toward happiness, and tuck bad incidents away, preferring to carry on as if nothing were wrong.

Sometimes I wish I shared that disposition.

Mina Harker's Journal

18 July.—It has been some time since I wrote in this little book. Six years, apparently. While Quincey was still a baby, I jotted down all my impressions of him, lest I forget. New motherhood is a splendid thing, or so what I wrote tells me. I recall more anxiety and exhaustion than I recorded.

Well! I shall begin again, now that I have news to share. Jack Seward has summoned us to visit him at Purfleet. Jonathan was determined to deny him. He takes his work so seriously these days, although, by the grim line of his mouth, the pallor that showed just briefly in his cheeks, and other signs that only I can detect, I understood that he wished to avoid the asylum and the old stamping-grounds of our monstrous foe. He is so sensitive now. Married life and a steady routine have allowed tender feelings to emerge, where once the demands of battle required hardiness of him.

I, however, am determined to go, and take Quincey with me. He is such a dear, independent boy, and solemnly promised Jonathan that he would look after me. No father could deny him, so off we go to spend the week! It is to be a grand summer adventure, of the kind Lucy and I used to have.

22 July.—*at Purfleet.* What a time we have had! Now that Quincey is tucked away in bed, I will write it all down. Here is

Jack's news: he's found a prospective wife among his own patients! Her name is Miss Gilda Fortescue, and she is the most charming friend—for I already consider her a friend. She is kind, and sweet, and—oh, I am ahead of myself.

Upon our arrival this afternoon, a glum orderly informed us that Dr. Seward was occupied with work, and would meet us for dinner. I put on my best charms and extracted a late lunch from the cook, for we were famished. Then Quincey and I went for a stroll in the gardens surrounding the asylum. They are lovely, done up cottage-style, with masses of roses blooming everywhere. Quincey raced about chasing butterflies, and told stories about everything he saw. He makes up such stupendous tales.

He had much to say about the tangle of growth on the other side of the fence. I promised him a ramble there tomorrow, even as I spied the crumbling stones of Carfax peering through the greenery. There can be no harm in walking there now. The Count is gone from the world.

We met Jack in his rooms at the appointed time. He isn't one of those stuffy men who refuses to dine with children. This is well, for it would go very hard on Quincey to be separated from his favourite "Uncle." The two of them get on like old chums. After a hearty embrace, they spoke of all the adventures they'd been up to since the last time we were together. I believe it has been more than two years! Too long.

As they spoke, Jack seemed to be full of nerves. His hands shook, and he glanced at me from time to time, appearing almost to blush. He looked quite young, fresh and full of life. I could barely look at him, for I recalled Lucy saying she thought he would make an excellent husband for me! This new, high energy of his appealed to me greatly. I could almost picture it myself!

He'd cleaned the place up, since the old days. A beautiful table was laid, with four place settings. The number didn't escape me. There was no need for a fire, since the evening was warm. The windows stood open to the glow of the golden hour. Outside, a trio of bats fluttered up into the sky, seeking insects to feed upon. This time is my favourite, when you can feel the night comingling with the day, tempering its harsher colours and bringing such peace.

There came a knock on the door. Jack leapt to open it, and ushered in a young woman I took at first for an angel. She is delicate and pale, all frothy curls and wide, earnest eyes. Such full lips! And a pleasing, round figure!

He introduced us, then dismissed the orderly who had, until that moment, accompanied her. What a sweet evening we had! We dined, and sipped wine, and talked about all sorts of things. The two of them kept no secrets, for Miss Fortescue told me straightaway that she was a patient, and dear Jack couldn't have hidden his feelings for her if he'd tried.

When Quincey began to droop in his chair, and his pudding spoon dropped onto the carpet, I took him to bed, with a promise to return so the grown-ups could have a proper talk.

I found the two of them tête-à-tête, their hands entwined, speaking in low whispers that couldn't be anything but love-talk. My heart is nearly bursting with happiness for Jack, and for dear Miss Fortescue as well!

They are engaged to be married. He has the approval of her family, and as he has no family remaining of his own, hers has adopted him already as their own son.

I must rest now, for the candle is disturbing Quincey's sleep. I hardly feel like resting. I am so happy!

Dr. Seward's Diary

22 July, late.—Gilda and I talked for some minutes after Mina left us, but I didn't dare keep her up, for fear of disturbing those dark forces that seem to overtake her at times. She confessed to being wrung out, poor dear, and to having a slight headache.

"Nowhere near as terrible as they have been," she assured me. "It bodes no evil."

It was a perfect evening, and Gilda was perfect, but her brain cannot always muster a long bout of concentration.

I admit that I feel a new optimism. We have done such good work together, and spoken of all sorts of things, shared our hearts and our histories. I can find nothing in her life to have caused such a shadow to fall upon her. I begin to hope that the source is in her nerves, and not in her brain tissue.

Mina's company has cheered us both, and built upon the steady improvements Gilda has seen during her time here. I have walked her to her room—adjacent to the guest quarters where Mina and young Quincey are staying. Gilda is an inmate no longer, but a dear guest as well, and soon to be a dweller in my rooms with me. I could nearly believe her to be entirely well. I will believe it. I do.

Mina Harker's Journal

23 July.—I hardly know where to start. It has been such a long and terrible day. It began well enough. Quincey and I slept in, waking to find the day clear and warm. Jack had long since gone to attend his patients, but Miss Fortescue greeted us in his sitting-room with a late breakfast. We lingered over tea and spoke of all sorts of things. There was only a little awkwardness between us, when she told me that Jack has hinted at great past adventures. She longs to learn more of them.

"You would tell me, if I asked," she said, her gentle voice high and sweet. "I know you were part of it, dear Mrs. Harker. You and your husband both! But I see from your looks that no, you wouldn't tell me unless you had Jack's permission. You're a good friend. I shall wait. But one day I will know, when Jack is sure I'm strong enough. I get stronger every day."

It was such a brave assertion, akin to Quincey's claims that he will soon outstrip his Papa in arm-wrestling.

Quincey grew restless, and demanded that I look out the window to see this bird, or such and such a butterfly, and once even a bat! I teased him over the last one, lest Miss Fortescue worry, and asked if she would accompany us for a walk. Oh, how I wish I had not asked! But one cannot know one's fate ahead of time. My life is ample proof of that.

We strolled arm-in-arm while Quincey ran ahead of us. Once or twice he caught a beetle or other insect in his hands. I made sure he released them unharmed.

We went further than I meant to, and soon came up against the fence where the grounds met with the wilder territory of Carfax. We stood among the carefully tended flowers, and peered at the neglected trees and waist-high weeds. I longed to visit the Count's old grounds, and revisit those days that marked the great before and after of my life. I couldn't ask such a thing of Miss Fortescue.

Before I could stop him, Quincey ran through a hole in the fence and darted off along a dusty track.

"Excuse me," I told Miss Fortescue. "I must go after him, or he'll be gone all afternoon."

I should have listened to the inward voice that said Quincey would be fine. I should have attended to her cry of distress, and returned her to safety before I charged through the fence. I would say it was a mother's care that compelled me, but there's no point in lying to these pages, which have already seen so much of tragedy and strangeness.

The idea of waiting for one more minute to cross over into Carfax vexed me. Seeing Quincey fly toward the crumbling stone, I couldn't help but follow.

I found him as I always do, via the silver thread that draws me to him wherever he may be, and has made him forbid me from playing hide and seek with him and his father. He'd crept into one of the buildings through a stuck-open door, and had stopped to admire a shaft of light coming down through a hole in the ceiling.

"Mama!" he cried, delighted to see me. "The earth! It sings!" He spun in a circle, arms thrown wide in ecstasy.

I immediately heard—or perhaps felt—the music of which he spoke. I can only describe it as tones, like bells ringing without being struck, arising from mounds of earth that stood here and there throughout the room. Broken, rotting boards lying strewn about awakened my memory: these mounds were the soil the Count brought from his home all those years ago, and which he'd used to make a refuge here in our country.

I should revile the scent of mouldering clay and all it repre-sented, but it sang to me so sweetly. I bent down and ran my hands through the earth. The Count had left his stamp upon my blood, his mark upon my soul, when he pressed my lips to the wound in his breast. Upon me, and upon the child that even then slept in my womb, as yet unbeknownst to me.

For his part, Quincey had begun to dig into one of the larger mounds, then flung himself upon his back and rolled in it until he was thoroughly coated. I laughed, and resisted the urge to rub some soil on my cheek.

He grew quite wild when I told him we must leave, and growled at me when I tried to take his hand. I had to be quite severe on him, and only called him back to his senses by promis-ing we would return and collect a jar of the soil for him to take home.

"Will the song come with it?" he asked.

Of course I had to say it would, or I would hear no end of it.

Back in the well-ordered garden once more, we found a dreadful scene. Miss Fortescue lay on the lawn, foam on her lips, her eyes staring blindly at the sky. A crowd of orderlies and one or two of the patients who were permitted to walk outside stood in a circle around her.

I rushed to her, and clutched her hand, which she gripped violently. "You're a devil!" she screamed, pointing at Quincey. "And your mother is a temptress! Vile demons!" She attempted to strike me, but I held her wrist.

"Dear Miss Fortescue," I whispered, all misery. "Come back to us, Miss Fortescue."

It was then that Jack came racing across the lawn, anxiety written on his features as he shouted at the crowd to disperse.

He wept as he stroked his beloved's hair, and assured me that the fit would pass, although it seemed to go on longer than he hoped. At last she stilled, sat up, and began to weep piteously.

The truth all came out afterwards in her room, while we tried to soothe her. Miss Fortescue is not well. A tumour of the brain, or so Jack has concluded, and who am I to doubt him? My heart breaks for her, and for him.

Dr. Seward's Diary

24 July.—Before the dawn. The little signs I had thought to dismiss—the tremor in her left hand, the way she sometimes stares as if seeing things—have returned in force, along with the emotional disturbance that today manifested so grotesquely.

Thank God for Mina! And even for young Quincey, for he did not flinch at Gilda's accusations, but held her hand most gently. Only Mina's voice seemed to calm her, and call her back from that far-flung land to which she alone travels.

We have been at her bedside non-stop. Even now, her brow is fevered, and her speech and manner sluggish. It is as if she moves under water. Her hands float in the air if we do not hold them.

24 July.—mid-morning. Something curious has occurred. I left Mina with Gilda while I stepped outside to smoke and clear my head. When I returned, the two of them were conversing merrily. It was the first spark of life I'd seen in my darling since the episode on the lawn.

Her lower lip, I daresay, was redder than usual. I caught a glimpse of a stain on Mina's blouse, just on the cuff, as if it had been dipped in red ink. Little Quincey—who had appeared to be sleeping on a sofa in the corner—sat up, and seemed, with his stare, to command me to silence, lest I disturb some ritual.

These are devilish thoughts. But her improvement! She took a cup of tea, and seemed to gain an impossible steadiness and strength. We tucked her in and told her to take her rest until noon. She went to sleep like a child, all softness and compliance, no hint of wildness at all.

I must think like a man of science, or rather, like a man of science who has witnessed the impossible, and knows it to exist.

Mina appears to have shared her blood with Gilda. That blood seems to have revived her.

Mina exhibits no signs of age, no wrinkles at the corners of her mouth, no crow's feet, no grey hairs.

She shares a rare bond with her son. They communicate without speech. I have seen her look at him, and he dash from the room and return with a bit of knitting for her to work at. It happened on their first night here. I noted it, but ascribed it to some habitual game they played together.

She walks during the day, attends church, and is as good a friend, and as good a lady, as any I know.

How are these things possible? Unless she is still vampire, or shares some quality of that dread spirit. Can it be all bad, when it dwells within her? Can it help my poor dear Gilda? Has it already helped her?

Mina Harker's Journal

24 July.—Afternoon. Oh dear. What have I done? All will out, if it hasn't already. It could not be helped. Where one has the means to assist a friend, one must.

—Evening. We have been through the fire, Jack and I, but what a different blaze from the one we suffered so many years ago. Then, we had a fight for our very souls; now, we strive for understanding.

He came to my room after lunch, and demanded that I tell him everything: what I had done, what I hoped to accomplish by it, and what I knew of my own condition. I replied in steady terms, and suggested that Miss Fortescue join us for our talk.

"Miss Fortescue!" he said. "This is a grave matter, is it not? Her nerves, Mina!"

I bit my lip, and almost couldn't keep from laughing, for she'd already recovered so well. Furthermore, I knew, in the same way that I always know where Quincey is, that she was standing right outside, listening at the keyhole. In a moment we heard her laughter like liquid music pouring in through the door, and she let herself in.

She was all cream and roses, her eyes bright and merry. She reported a slight headache, but begged most earnestly to join us.

"I should like to understand as well as you, Jack, what miracle Mina has wrought."

First, Jack examined her, and found there were still some signs of disease. The tremor in her hand has not disappeared. She exhibits some difficulties in picking up a pen and writing her name. I was not surprised, for, as I told him, I'd only placed a single drop of blood on her lip.

"And how did you arrive at the idea that you should do it?" he asked, pen poised over notebook.

Now that I was dealing with the scientist more than the lover, I knew I could confess all. He knows my connection with the Count. He witnessed, along with Dr. Van Helsing, Arthur Holmwood, and Quincey Morris, that shameful ritual of blood-drinking which the villain forced upon me. I reminded him of it.

"He wished for me to be like him," I said.

He gazed at me with a fevered look. "We knew as much. But that ended when we killed him."

"So we thought. His voice no longer sounded in my mind, and I could endure the touch of holy objects. But you never knew the sequel," I told him. "Besides Jonathan and I, only Dr. Van Helsing knows of it."

"Van Helsing!"

I saw I had his full attention. Miss Fortescue, who understands me now on a blood-level, gripped my hand with welcome sympathy.

"Once we came home from that dread adventure, I discovered I was with child. Thus Jonathan and I found joy amid the sorrows our ordeal had wrought."

"As did we all," he said.

I fixed him with a steady look. "My labour ran long, and I suffered much loss of blood. For some moments after Quincey was born, I ceased to breathe. Dr. Van Helsing revived me, for he'd arrived, in that way of his, just in time. Do you know how he did it?"

Sweet Gilda answered. "A drop of Quincey's blood."

The darling girl was right, of course.

"I don't completely understand it," I said. "Call it an infection, call it a force, a will of its own that worked through the Count—it was in me, and concentrated in Quincey. Dr. Van Helsing pierced his fingertip with a needle, and used his blood to revive me."

I paused, remembering awakening to heat on my lips, and feeling as if I had been born anew.

"Dr. Van Helsing stayed with us for some weeks, Jack, and kept a watchful eye on us. He never would have said so to Jonathan, but he feared for me, feared I would become like that beast who took our dear Lucy from us. He feared, too, for Quincey, although he didn't say it. You've seen how he always pays particular attention to him, dandles him on his knee when we're all together. He's checking him for faults. I know it, but I don't fear any longer. We are—different. Better, I would say."

"And entirely good." Jack echoed my thoughts on the matter. "Will you age?" He watched Gilda as he asked. I knew why: she was so beautiful with her golden hair and full cheeks. It is a dream, is it not? To remain so?

"Quincey grows, as you see. As for me, I'm not sure. Our middle years are long, and unless illness fells us, nothing much seems to change until age creeps in. Perhaps my life will be longer than most. Such things are a mystery, I'm afraid."

He took Gilda's hand. "If she is well," he told me, "there's nothing for me to fear. I'm sure Jonathan feels the same."

I made no reply to this.

We have written to Van Helsing to ask for his blessing, and to invite him to the wedding. It will take place as soon as may be. I'll stay on to prepare, of course—for the ceremony and party, and to make certain Gilda is entirely well.

"You really are willing?" Jack said to me. "You would do this for us?"

I told him the absolute truth: to have a sister is my dearest wish. My heart is so full, I can hardly keep from shaking as I write! A sister! As dear Lucy was, and always should have been.

Letter, Abraham Van Helsing, M. D., D. Ph., D. Lit., etc., etc., to Dr. Seward.

26 July

My Friend,—

How wonderful to receive your telegram.

Rest assured that good Madame Mina did indeed die on the day when she birth our brave young Quincey, who came from her womb with teeth already growing through his gums. What does that tell you, friend Jack, about this child? You have seen how wise he is, how fast he grow, how he walk and speak long before other children his same age.

That good lady! In her so great wisdom she refuse all attention from the midwife and any doctor, and calls instead upon me. Do you see, friend Jack, how the un-life works through her? The mother's body holds the child within her, and, when all goes well, does not reject it as it should, as foreign matter. In her womb, Quincey knows not what is good or bad, only that the Count's blood come through her, so he fold that blood into his own in a new way. What miracle this holds I know not, but Madame Mina is no monster, nor will your Gilda be.

I need not tell you how I grieved after I killed those three so beautiful brides of the Count. When Madame Mina birth young Quincey, and the life flowed out from her, I said, Death, you shall not have her! It was love that cause me to prick the baby's finger and put it in her mouth. She only take a small sip from him, but the colour flowed into her cheeks and I knew all was well. Trust her blood to do the same for your Miss Gilda.

I shall be there soon as I may to wish you joy. Our friend Arthur Holmwood and his so-sweet Lady Beatrice will not, alas, attend your wedding. He passed through Amsterdam just as your telegram arrive, and cannot return to England on time. He said he might arrange it so, but I dissuade him. If Miss Gilda look so much like Miss Lucy Westenra, it is for the best he not meet her yet.

Van Helsing.

Jonathan Harker's Journal

26 July.—There is to be a wedding. I have wished Jack joy, and I have packed my things. Soon I'll join Mina in that place. Of all the places in England, it holds my darkest secrets.

The soil sings to me. It is a dark song, with no joy in it. What the Count did to me I have not told a soul, not even this journal. To claim my memory was blank was better, much better, than to admit that I recall the press of his teeth to my wrist, and the feeling of his kiss upon my lips.

I have my jar of flies for the journey. They will keep my strength up, and keep my blood full of life for when I see my family again. Mina will be hungry after all these days apart, unless she's found someone else to feed upon.

I will tear out these pages and burn them. No: she knows how I feel. She can read my thoughts. If I write them here, perhaps I need not think such things in her company. Her company: as if I can be free of it! She could sense the Count over vast expanses, so I suppose there's no hiding.

Nor should there be, for she is always good. I know just what she'll say. "These little misunderstandings are common in marriage." She'll kiss my cheek, and forgive my resentful thoughts.

What of Miss Gilda Fortescue? The very name raises dread in me. She is to receive the blood, Mina's blood, and be closer to her than I have ever been.

Jack will have to feed her, to learn all that I know. One keeps one's veins open. One readies oneself. One offers oneself, eats liver to restore the blood, eats living things to restore the life in the blood.

If Gilda is to be Mina's sister, then Jack shall be my brother. A brotherhood, as it was in the old days. We were bold and brave then; now we must be resigned. I know my role, and he shall know his.

There. I am decided. I am resigned.

Elizabeth Twist lives in Hamilton, Ontario, where she untames a garden and teaches meditation. Her stories have appeared in NonBinary Review, Fiends in the Furrows II, and Unfettered Hexes, among others. Find her on Twitter @elizabethtwist.

Quincey P. Morris
The Enigmatic Texan
By Chris McAuley

Imagine a figure stepping out of the shadows of an old, dusty legend, a man who brings with him the whispers of prairies and the howl of wild frontiers. Quincey P. Morris, a name that dances on the edges of Bram Stoker's *Dracula*, is one such figure. He appears, larger than life, a rugged Texan amidst the fog and foreboding of Victorian England. But who is he really? What secrets does he hold, and why does his story matter? This is an exploration of Quincey P. Morris, a character as enigmatic and fascinating as the tale he inhabits.

Quincey P. Morris strides into the narrative like a gust of wind from the open plains, a man of action and mystery. Described as an all-American adventurer, he captures the imagination with his broad shoulders and confident demeanor. Stoker's description paints him vividly: "He is a man of medium height, strongly built, with his shoulders set back over a broad, deep chest and a neck well balanced on the trunk as the head is on the neck." It's a portrait of a man who is both grounded and ready to spring into action, a living, breathing embodiment of the American frontier spirit.

Quincey embodies the archetypal American hero, a figure forged in the fires of adventure and rugged individualism. He stands in stark contrast to his more reserved British companions, bringing a breath of fresh, untamed air into the story. His cowboy background is not just a quirk; it shapes his every move and decision. Quincey's courage and loyalty are the stuff of legends, traits that make him both endearing and formidable. He is a man who faces danger head-on, with a heart full of bravery and a soul steeped in the spirit of the wild West.

Quincey's unrequited love for Lucy Westenra adds a layer of poignancy to his character. He loves her quietly, with a strength that speaks volumes even when words fail him. His heartbreak is a silent echo in the story, a testament to his deep feelings and his respect for her happiness. Unlike the other suitors, Quincey's love is marked by a selfless nobility, a willingness to stand aside for the sake of her joy. His relationship with Lucy also highlights the cultural contrasts within the narrative. While Arthur Holmwood is the epitome of English nobility and Dr. Seward the learned scholar, Quincey is the untamed spirit, the passionate heart, and the exotic allure of the American frontier.

Quincey serves a particular role within the retinue of Stoker's vampire hunters, he's the 'muscle', the action man who complements the intellectual strategies of Van Helsing and the medical knowledge of Dr. Seward. But he is more than just brawn; his practical knowledge and frontier experience are invaluable. Quincey's familiarity with danger and his readiness to act decisively often propel the group forward. In the climactic chase to stop Dracula, it is Quincey's relentless pursuit and courage that become crucial. His death, while tragic, is the ultimate act of heroism, a self-sacrifice that underscores the novel's themes of bravery and loyalty.

The character is also rich with symbolic significance. His presence in the novel reflects the 19th century fascination with the Wild West and its larger-than-life heroes. Bram Stoker also made Quincey's character a critique of this mythos. His untamed nature, while admirable, also highlights the perils of unbridled individualism. His death also serves a purpose in mythological critique, a symbolic reconciliation between the Old World and the New, a union forged through sacrifice and common purpose.

There are also similarities between Quincey and Dracula, they are both outsiders but represent the opposite ends of the moral spectrum. Quincey represents the positive force, the outsider who brings fresh perspectives and new energy. Dracula on the other hand, is the corrupting influence, the dark invader. While Dracula seeks to pervert the natural order of life and death, Quincey embraces his mortality, sacrificing himself for the greater good. This contrast highlights the thematic battle between good and evil, light and dark, mortality and the undead. These aspects of life particularly interested Bram Stoker in his life and linked to his fascination with Christian theology and the occult.

Quincey is a mysterious individual in the mythos of the Dracula universe. Perhaps this is linked to the underdeveloped nature of his character. He's more a symbol of American bravado than a fully realized individual. His background and motivations are hinted at but never fully explored, leaving him somewhat enigmatic. Additionally, his dialogue, marked by exaggerated American slang, can verge on the stereotypical, reducing him at times to a caricature.

I've been very keen to develop the nature of our mysterious Texan within and also outside the StokerVerse. Both Dacre and I see him as one of our favourite characters and that's mostly linked to his death. It's one of the novel's most memorable and poignant moments. As he lies dying, he grasps his friends' hands and says, "It was worth this to die! Look! Look! The sun is rising!" This scene encapsulates the novel's themes of sacrifice, friendship, and the triumph of good over evil. In this way Quincey's legacy extends beyond the pages of Dracula, inspiring various interpretations and adaptations. In these retellings, his character is often given more depth and focus. For examples of these I would point to *Azeman, or the Testament of Quincey Morris* by Lisa Moore and *Quincey Morris, Vampire* by P.N. Elrod.

The adaptations of the character in film feature some of the most interesting interpretations through the decades. In the earliest Dracula-centric films, Quincey Morris was often conspicuously absent. Movies like the 1931 Universal Pictures *Dracula* starring Bela Lugosi chose to streamline the story, focusing primarily on the core conflict between Dracula and Van Helsing. Quincey's character, with his American roots and cowboy persona, was seen as less integral to the European gothic aesthetic these early films sought to capture. This changed in 1970, with *Count Dracula* directed by Jesus Franco and starring Christopher Lee featuring a robust portrayal of Quincey by Jack Taylor. Although the character was still slightly one-dimensional, it began to hint at the adventurous and courageous aspects of his nature. But the most significant portrayal of Quincey Morris comes in Francis Ford Coppola's *Bram Stoker's Dracula* in 1992. Played by Billy Campbell, Quincey is depicted as the quintessential American cowboy, complete with rugged charm and a penchant for heroism. This version of Quincey captures the spirit of the original character while also adding layers of complexity and depth. Campbell's portrayal highlights Quincey's bravery, loyalty, and the poignant unrequited love for Lucy Westenra. This film firmly re-establishes Quincey Morris as an essential part of the Dracula narrative.

Quincey's character speaks to the enduring human fascination with heroism, adventure, and the triumph over darkness. His journey, from the American West to the heart of Dracula's lair, is a testament to the power of courage and solidarity in the face of insurmountable odds. This universal appeal transcends the boundaries of time and culture, making Quincey P. Morris an indispensable part of the Dracula narrative and a beloved figure among fans. His legacy as a courageous, loyal, and selfless hero ensures that he will always hold a special place in the hearts of those who delve into the dark and captivating world of Bram Stoker's Dracula.

Chris McAuley is a best-selling, award-winning writer who is most famous for creating the popular StokerVerse franchise with Dacre Stoker (Bram Stoker's great grand-nephew). This continuation of Bram's work has proliferated from graphic novels, books, audio dramas, table-top games into the world of television and film. He has also created a successful science fiction franchise with Hollywood actress Claudia Christian (star of *Babylon 5*) called *Dark Legacies*. Chris has recently been nominated for the highest award for writing in tabletop games—The Ennies for his Three Musketeers vs Chthulu RPG which has also become a comic book series. He is also known for his work on *Doctor Who*, *Star Trek*, *Star Wars*, *Battlestar Galactica*, and *Terminator* franchises. Away from writing duties he is the co-owner of X-G3 Productions, a film company spearheaded by CNN's George J Giakoumis and Peter S Gialoumis as well as a multiple award-winning Executive Producer on The Stranded Warrior Sci-Fi film.

He loves *Dracula Beyond Stoker* and believes that if Bram was around today he would love to see how talented writers have been dipping into his creation and creating original stories.

How Quincey P. Morris Lost His Finest Horse and Found His Way To England
By Kay Hanifen

Letter to Lucy Westenra
(written on the train to Bucharest)

My Darling Miss Lucy,

You always loved the stories I told you about my life in America and the wild, untamed wilderness of Texas. And I loved to tell them. Most of them, anyway. There's one I never told you for fear that it would terrify you and change the way you look at me. Now, though, I keep going back to it and wondering if things would have turned out different if I did tell you. Maybe… maybe I could have stopped that no-good bloodsucking varmint from taking you from us and kept Miss Mina from becoming that monster's next intended victim. Even now, I can only tell it in the form of a letter to a dead friend, one only to be opened in the event of my own end.

If I voiced these fears to our dear friends, I'm certain that they'd tell me I've been acting a fool for thinking that the events I'm about to relate would change their opinion of me in any way. They know a part of it, at least, just that a blood sucking vampire bat killed one of my prize horses. Not sure why I said it was in the Pampas. It sounds foolish, but I don't want the memory of my home sullied any more than it already is. Saying it happened on another continent gave me just enough distance to even mention the incident out loud. But what I told them ain't even the half of it, not by a long shot.

I figure I should start at the very beginning. You remember how I was raised by my grandpappy after my pa disappeared. Grandpappy fought in the war for Texas's independence. They called him One-Shot Bob on account of his sharpshooting. The man could hit a hummingbird from across a field. When Texas joined the Union, he put down his gun and made a name for himself as a rancher, owning one of the largest cattle ranches in the state. He found himself a nice wife and they had plenty of kids, all with the same knack for shooting.

My pa was one of the best gunmen north of the Rio Grande, but that didn't stop him from catching an early death out in the desert. I don't know what killed him. Sometimes, I wonder if it's the same demon that took everything else.

My ma died a little after I was born, so after Pa disappeared, Granny and Grandpappy raised me to be a cattleman like he was. I've told you stories from that happy time.

When I was a boy, Grandpappy would take me through the desert, just him, me, the horses, and the grazing cattle for months at a time. Sure, we'd stop in small towns every once in a while to gather supplies or sleep on a real bed, but I spent most of my boyhood sleeping under the endless stars, lulled to dreamland by the stories my grandpappy would tell about the world that he'd learned from the Apache folks he often traded with and the legends behind the constellations. He taught me to navigate with just the stars as a guide so that I'd never get lost like my pa.

Those were the best days of my life. Our family thrived both on the ranch and among the townsfolk. We were respected members of the community, and our little corner of Texas had become something of a paradise. Even now, I smile when I think back on those days, though the memories are tainted by the horrors to come.

It started with Grandpappy's disappearance. The man was a stubborn old fool, one that didn't seem to know how to die. At least, that's how he was to me—immortal and strong despite his gnarled hands and weatherbeaten face. I suppose we're all children in that way. We never seem to be able to accept the frailty of those who raise us, assuming that they'll live forever even when we know that's not true.

But Grandpappy was not the type to spend his twilight years sitting on the porch drinking sweet tea and watching his small empire work, bustling about like colonies of ants. Even in his old age, he still went out herding cattle and sleeping under the stars, much to Granny's consternation.

One night, he didn't return when we expected him back. We waited a day. And then two. We thought, perhaps, that he'd been thrown off his horse or was attacked by a coyote. As the night sky faded into darkness and the stars began to emerge on the second day, I decided that I'd had enough waiting. So, I slung my shotgun around my shoulder and headed out. Granny tried to talk me into bringing my favorite ranch hand, Bill Marsten, with me, but I declined. It would take too long to rouse him from his cabin and wait for him to get ready, so it was better for me to go on my own.

"Wait!" Granny called the moment I stepped through the door. She emerged carrying a silver cross on a chain. "For comfort and protection. The Lord and Jesus are with you, always."

After putting it around my neck, I gave her a kiss on the cheek. "I'll be back with Grandpappy faster than you can shoot the wings off a skeeter."

She stepped back, her eyes crinkling in a soft smile. "You'd better, boy."

Grandpappy told us that he was taking the cattle to Goldwater River to let them drink and graze. He'd been there a million times before, and aside from the occasional snake or predator that needed scaring off, it wasn't particularly dangerous. But still, with the image of my grandpappy dead from being thrown off his horse or languishing with a rattler bite at the forefront of my mind, I hastily saddled my palomino stallion, Dusty, and raced to the river.

But I didn't need to go so far as all that. Grandpappy was walking on the path scarcely a mile from the house. I say walked, but that's not right. He limped and lurched like a dying man. A stream of blood trickled down his neck, forming canyons out of the dust and dirt that covered him.

"Whoa!" I brought my horse to a halt near him. "Grandpappy, are you alright? What happened?"

He barely acknowledged me, instead staring out at the darkening horizon and muttering to himself. I dismounted my horse to better meet his eyes.

"Alright, Grandpappy, I'll help you into the saddle and we'll walk home. Granny has a massive stew on the pot and my stomach is grumbling. Ready? One…two…three." On three, I hoisted him onto the horse's back, much like what he did for me when I was too small to mount on my own. I led him back to the ranch where Granny waited.

"Good Lord in Heaven, what happened to him?" she asked, racing to meet us as we approached.

"I haven't the foggiest clue. He was like this when I found him." I explained everything to her as I helped him to dismount Dusty.

"Well, don't just stand there. Get him inside and get him cleaned up. I'll send for Doctor Grey." Though she was usually content to let her husband take charge, my granny was a woman as steely as Grandpappy when she had to be. There's something about the wilds of Texas that takes the woman out of folks. It tests your mettle, and only the strong survive. Miss Mina reminds me of her sometimes. They're both as tough and smart as the menfolk around them, and we'd all be wiser to listen to them more.

You, though, awakened something in me that I never would have found in the wilderness: tenderness. Lucy, you were not the bravest or the strongest, but you were the kindest person I'd ever met in this cruel world. I wanted to protect that light and enjoy your warmth. But your heart always belonged to another.

I suppose that, since we're in the business of confessing right now and I plan to chuck this letter straight into the fire, I should tell you that my heart didn't always belong to you. For a time, it belonged to Bill Marsten. When you spend weeks on end with just one other man, the cattle, and the stars, with no woman in sight, you grow very close to that man. Bill was no exception. The nights we spent together made me feel in much the same way I felt about you. It may be unnatural, but it's the God's honest truth. I've had enough of secrets and lies, even if it's lies to protect others. Miss Mina has proven how dangerous those lies can be.

But I've wandered off the trail again, haven't I? Miss Lucy, I don't know how you could tolerate my stories with all the ways they wander here and there like cattle grazing on the plains. You were always an incredibly patient soul.

So, I took Grandpappy to the back bedroom and got him settled while Granny heated a pot of water. When she appeared in the doorway, I got up to leave. But then, I felt a vice-like grip on my arm. Grandpappy stared up at me, his eyes as wide and wild as a horse cornered by wolves.

"Grandpappy?" I said, gently prying his fingers from my arm and cradling his hand in mine. "Grandpappy, can you hear me?"

"It's still out there," he gasped. "It won't stop until it's destroyed everything."

"What's out there?" I shifted, knocking the cross loose from beneath my shirt. Grandpappy shuddered and raised his wrinkled arms as though to protect himself from the pendant hanging from my neck.

"No, no, no, no, no," he cried.

I backed away as though I'd been burned. Granny rested a hand on my shoulder. "Mary went to fetch the doctor. I can take it from here."

I nodded. "Maybe you can get some sense out of him. In the meantime, I'll find Bill and we'll rustle up a party."

"You will do no such thing. Not until morning anyway."

Reaching for my gun again, I shook my head. "The trail might go cold. The longer I wait here, the harder it will be to find this thing."

"Because going out in the middle of the night half-cocked and with a posse of exhausted men will make finding whoever or whatever attacked your grandpappy so much easier." She stood on her tiptoes to rap on my forehead with her knuckles. "Use your common sense, boy. Get some sleep and get started first thing in the morning."

As much as I wanted to get out there and find whoever did this to my grandpappy, Granny was right. Going out there without a plan could make me wind up just like Pa. I sighed, admitting defeat. "Wake me as soon as the sun rises."

True to her word, Granny got me as soon as the sun poked its yellow head up on the eastern horizon. I saddled Dusty, got my rifle, and headed to Bill's cabin. It was only about two miles yonder, so I made quick time. Bill, who was usually up with the cock's grow, was still asleep when I pounded on the door.

When he opened it, he looked sickly and unnaturally pale. Dark circles had formed under his eyes, and he was still in his bedclothes. "What're you doing here?" he asked, his demeanor unusually gruff. The man could be quiet, but he always welcomed me, even when I paid unannounced visits.

I furrowed my brows with concern. "Well, I was going to ask for your help tracking the varmint that attacked my grandpappy, but now that I'm looking at you, I'm beginning to think I should be looking somewhere else for help. What happened to you?"

He produced a handkerchief from his pocket and coughed into it. "I'm fine. Just a little sick is all. You said that something attacked your Grandpappy? What was it?"

"I don't know," I replied, and told him the events of the night before. When I finished, he somehow seemed even paler than when he first opened the door. "You ever heard of anything like this?"

His bloodless face went grim. "I reckon I have. Give me some time to get ready, and we'll find the varmint's trail."

"I was thinking of rustling up a posse."

He shook his head and went back inside. "We'll have the element of surprise if it's just the two of us. These things are wilier than a cornered coyote and twice as dangerous. We have to move now."

"What are they?" I asked.

He ignored me, turning his back and grabbing the nearest shirt—one probably discarded from the night before—and threw it on along with a pair of chaps and his Stetson. Slinging his rifle over his shoulder, he faced me, the hat shadowing his gaze. "I don't rightly know what they're called, but I've met one before. They're unholy demons who spread their evil like disease upon the living. But they only come out at night, so we have to find it before we lose daylight."

He brushed past me, heading to the stable. I'll admit that I was a tad unsettled. I'd only seen Bill a week before, and he was as hale and hearty as ever, but his joviality was now replaced by a grim countenance and a sickly frame. This was a marked change in my—my dearest friend, and I didn't know what to do with it. Naturally, I was worried, but he seemed loathe to talk about it.

When we reached Goldwater River, the cattle were all gone. The hoofprints they left implied a kind of stampede, but there wasn't any indication as to what might've frightened them away. I could find no signs of wolves or coyotes anywhere, and I didn't know what else might have caused them to vanish without a trace.

"Come on. We're losing daylight," Bill said, but his voice sounded funny. It was like he was talking, but someone else was putting the words in his mouth.

"You never told me about these things before," I said, riding up beside him.

Bill seemed to be looking for something, but I couldn't tell what. "Weren't none of your business," he practically growled.

My eyebrows shot up. He had never spoken like that to me before. Something was wrong. "It became my business when it attacked my grandpappy. So, tell me everything you know."

He was silent for a long while. Though he was usually a man of few words, this reticence to speak was strange for him. It felt as though an unnatural pall had fallen upon us both. His shoulders shook, and I took my eyes off the road ahead to get a good look at his face.

Tears streamed down his cheeks, and his jaw looked tight enough to break in two. His breathing now seemed forcibly even, and he was as still as a cornered rabbit.

"Bill, what's going on?" I asked.

"I can't get his voice outta my head," he whispered. He turned to me, the whites of his eyes gone red. "I can't hold him back much longer. Quincey, you have to run and keep running until the ranch is far behind you."

"I ain't going nowhere. Not until you tell me what's happening."

He let out a low groan before drawing his rifle. "Go. Now."

"Whatever this is, we can fight it. Together. Just talk to me."

"He won't let me," Bill gritted out, his face twisting with agony. Raising the gun, he fired it into the air. Taking advantage of my surprise and Dusty's spook, he spurred his horse and galloped off.

I figured that he would lead me to whoever did this to him and Grandpappy, so I gave chase. He rode his poor horse hard, forcing me to keep pace at Dusty's expense.

When we reached Joelson's Mesa, he dismounted and vanished among the crags and crevices. I halted Dusty. The gelding's sides heaved, and white foam flecked his lips. Bill was gone, and if I wanted to get us both back, the horses needed tending.

I dismounted and grabbed Dusty's reins with one hand and his horse's reins in the other. There was a small creek a little way back, so I led them to it. While the horses drank their fill, I wracked my brain to think of what to do next. Bill was acting like a man possessed. If I wanted to get him back and help Grandpappy, I needed to know what I was up against. Figuring he would return for his horse, I stayed with the animals until the sun started to go down and the desert heat gave way to its wintry chill.

I tied up the horses and built myself a fire nearby, keeping them well within the radius of warmth and light. A bat flew overhead as dusk gave way to pitch darkness.

Though I tried to stay awake and wait for Bill to come to his senses, my eyelids drooped. A gentle mist formed around me, and I wondered where it might have come from. We don't get mist in the desert, but here it was dancing at the edge of the firelight. I tried to stay awake, but the mesmerizing movements sent me drifting into a deep sleep.

I woke to someone shaking my arm. Bill's face hovered over me, his eyes wide with terror. "Get up. Take my horse and go like you should have done in the first place."

I blinked blearily, not quite understanding his meaning. "What?"

And then I heard a heavy thud. Scrambling to a sitting position, my eyes met Dusty's terrified gaze. He had collapsed and his sides heaved but he seemed unwilling or unable to move. And attached to his neck like a leech was the biggest bat I'd ever seen. I watched in paralyzed horror as the heaving of Dusty's sides slowed to a stop and his eyes went vacant.

The spell broke. "I'll kill you for that, you sonofabitch!" I shouted, drawing my pistol.

The bat picked up its blood-soaked head and screeched, barreling towards me. But Bill got in the way, grabbing the bat and trying to wrestle it into submission. "Run!"

I shot it, the bullet tearing a hole in its massive black wings. The creature was undeterred, latching onto Bill like a babe at its mother's teat and refusing to let go. I pulled the trigger again, but the rest of the chamber was empty. A pile of bullets glinted in the moonlight nearby. Someone had removed them from my six-shooter's chambers, all but the one already loaded. With a battle cry, I charged, trying to yank the demon off him.

"Quincey, leave me," Bill choked out.

Adjusting my grip on its leathery shoulders, I grit my teeth and pulled. "I ain't letting you go."

The creature's wings shot out, striking me in the chest and sending me flying nearly ten feet away. Bill's horse, already terrified, whinnied and pulled at his reins. Every day, I thank my lucky stars for the miracle that he stayed tied up. It might not have done much in the end, but it helped buy me time and distance. I probably would have died otherwise.

As I lay there winded and catching my breath, the bat's red eyes met mine and it smiled, revealing long, needle-sharp fangs.

And then it snapped Bill's neck.

I didn't scream or cry out. I didn't even weep. I simply untied the reins and mounted his horse. The poor critter was more than happy to sprint as far away from the demon as possible. Even with the wind buffeting my ears, I could hear the sound of leathery wings and the screeches of the creature flying overhead. We rode like that for miles, the demon following above without actually attacking. After a while, I realized the horrible truth. It was toying with me, letting the horse get tired and giving me a false hope, and soon, it would go in for the kill.

As soon as I had this realization, the demon decided that it was done playing. It dove and slammed into me, knocking me off the horse's back. There were a couple dull snaps and then I was hit with a paroxysm of blinding pain. It tore my breath away. The creature went for my throat, just like it did with Bill. But then it recoiled as though it had been burned and let out another inhuman screech. This one, though, sounded more like frustration than the thrill of the hunt.

My hand went for my throat as it backed away, and I felt the silver cross around my neck. Forcing myself to sit up, I held out the cross in full view of the demon. Once again, it was repelled by a symbol of the holiest sacrifice.

"Get back!" I shouted. "Don't you come any nearer, demon."

It hissed but retreated, so I forced myself to my feet. The horse was long gone, but as long as I had the cross, the evil wouldn't dare touch me. With every muscle and bone in my body protesting, I slowly began to limp back home. Any time I sensed the creature sneak too close, I would brandish my cross and it would back away.

Using the stars to guide me, I walked all through the night. As the moon gave way to the break of day, the devil vanished, leaving me alone, injured, and exhausted in the warming desert sun.

The ranch was eerily quiet when I finally limped through the gates. The cows and heifers were lowing, waiting to be milked, and the chickens clucked for their breakfast.

"Granny? Grandpappy?" I shouted, my voice hoarse from the screaming and hours spent in the desert without anything to soothe my parched throat. Stumbling to the pump, I got myself a drink of the cool water, a balm to my soul after the night of horrors. It revived me a bit, just enough to go looking for them.

Lord, I wish I hadn't. All the servants were dead, their necks snapped and their bodies drained of blood. I found each of them in their beds without any signs of struggle, and I couldn't tell if they died there or if the devil who did this had posed them afterwards.

Because there were signs of struggle and blood on the walls in the other rooms, I suspected that it was the latter rather than the former. "Granny! Grandpappy!" I cried, my search becoming more frantic as I rushed from room to room.

They were in the bedroom, curled in each other's arms. For a moment, I thought they were asleep, but then I saw the wounds on Granny's throat and the way her dull, vacant eyes stared at nothing. I stepped closer, my foot falling on a squeaky floorboard. Grandpappy's eyes snapped open, and he stared at me. It wasn't my grandpappy anymore. The demon that took his form glared at me with such utter loathing and contempt that I staggered out of the room. He did not pursue. With that information and the fact that the bat demon only seemed to attack at night, I figured that these creatures rested in the daytime. I knew what I had to do.

With a cold finality, I opened the safe where Grandpappy kept his money and Granny kept her jewels and packed them away in a bag full of supplies. Then, I set loose all the animals, saving a horse for myself and the ride ahead. My ribs were definitely broken, as was my collarbone. I was in no fit state to walk.

Once the animals were taken care of, I poured all our oil and kerosene through the house. With a final prayer for the souls of those inside, I lit a match and dropped it. The house went up like dry tinder. An eerie, inhuman scream ululated from the master bedroom. I turned my back to it, mounted my horse, and rode to Houston.

When I got there, my body gave out. The injuries I sustained in the fight and the days of riding were just too much for me. For weeks, I was laid up in bed with fever while doctors and nurses guarded me around the clock. It took another several weeks for me to feel well enough to travel, and by then, I wanted to get as far away from Texas as possible.

The rest, as you know, is history.

Jonathan has related that something similar happened to him when he escaped that dread Count's castle. What we saw and experienced was just too much for the mind and body to take.

I've thought about confiding in him about what happened to me. Out of all our friends, he was the one who would most likely understand. But I fear, Miss Lucy, that I am a coward at heart. I fear that if I tell this story, he and the rest will think differently of me. After all, I should have recognized the signs of what you were becoming, but I didn't want to believe it. Thinking of those awful days is like putting your hand in hot coals. All it will do is hurt. I didn't want to believe that the monster from the desert had somehow followed me across the ocean to torment me once more.

But it wasn't my monster this time. My silence got you killed and now risks Miss Mina's soul and the lives of countless others. For that, I beg your forgiveness. I failed you just like I failed Grandpappy, Granny, Bill, and all our servants. But I solemnly swear to you, Miss Lucy, that I will not fail this time. I love our friends as you have loved them, and I will gladly lay my life down for each and every one.

Wherever you are, I beg that you pray for my soul, and I will do the same for you.

Love Always,
Quincey P. Morris

Kay Hanifen was born on a Friday the 13th and once lived for three months in a haunted castle. So, obviously, she had to become a horror writer. Her work has appeared in over fifty anthologies and magazines. When she's not consuming pop culture with the voraciousness of a vampire at a 24-hour blood bank, you can usually find her with her black cats or at:

kayhanifenauthor.wordpress.com.

The Real Adventures of Quincey Morris
By Doris V. Sutherland

QUINCEY
Your own greed got you here, Malone.

MEAN MALONE
Quincey Morris! You wouldn't leave me hanging over this abandoned mineshaft, would you?

QUINCEY
No, I'm not heartless like you. But I can't pull you up until you lose the gold nuggets.

MEAN MALONE
Lose my nuggets? Why, you varmint!

"Bloody hell," mumbled Barry Kitching. "Who writes this stuff?"

Well, somebody who went to Hollywood with dreams of working alongside Cecil B. DeMille or John Ford but who ended up scripting *Quincey Morris* cartoons instead. That poor bugger wrote it, and Barry had to draw it.

Still, he'd been given decent storyboards: those Western towns and cactus-filled deserts carried a certain nostalgia. And at least he was doing the keyframes. How he pitied the young animators stuck with the in-betweens.

One of those youngsters came up behind him.

"Uh, just so ya know, Mr. Kitching, the first few episodes are done," said the boy, whose name was Lew. "Y'know, with sound and everything. We're having a projection."

"Oh, right, I'll be over." Barry was left pondering how the prospect of seeing a completed cartoon had once been a satisfying conclusion rather than just another chore.

Quincey Morris was on the screen, square-jawed and dot-eyed. The sheriff greeted him.

"Hey," said Lew. "You drew the sheriff tipping his chair back, like someone would in real life!"

"Well, yeah," said Barry. *Dear God. Was that sort of detail really so novel to these younger animators?*

The only animation in the next scenes concerned the characters' mouths, and even that disappeared when the masked bandits turned up.

A slideshow, thought Barry. *I'm making bloody slideshows.*

The villains tied up Quincey Morris, but since that was too complex for tightly-scheduled animation, all the cartoon showed was the baddies holding a bit of rope while the camera panned to the background. (A nice background, granted. Diana always painted good deserts.) Quincey cut his way free with his trusty bowie knife and punched out the dastardly villains. Cartoon over. That's all, folks.

"Bloody awful," grumbled Barry.

"Come off it," said Dennis, another youngster. "What do you expect from telly cartoons?" Dennis had a tidy shirt, neat hair and thick glasses, which made Barry wonder if he got picked on by his hipper peers.

And the lad was quite right, Barry reminded himself. No animator was at their best when working for television, especially not US television. Just look at Halas & Batchelor: they were the Walt Disney of Britain, once. The old, good Walt Disney, who had Satan awakening to *Night on Bare Mountain*. But now they were more like Blighty's answer to Hanna-Barbera, reduced to making stuff the US studios couldn't be bothered with. Barely-animated cartoons about the Osmonds and the Jackson Five, existing to sell enough toys for the investors to stay happy. This studio was no better. Goodbye, golden age; hello, nineteen-seventies.

Barry watched the youngsters striding back to their desks. Never mind *drawing* for Hanna-Barbera: with their primary-coloured outfits and crazy hairstyles, they could've starred in those cheap American cartoons. The girls applied make-up the way animators painted on cels, while the boys' facial hair looked like sketchbook scribbling. And their conversation! It set Barry's teeth on edge. Were they competing to use the word "like" as many times as possible?

He had to remind himself that, had he married and started a family, his kids would've been no different.

Plus, he was separate from the youngsters. The studio was an old, oddly-shaped building where every large room had a sort of half-room squeezed into its corner. He'd ensured that his desk was inside one such cubby-hole, like a cubicle in an American office. Not that this prevented the occasional visitor.

"Uh, can I borrow your book again, Mr. Kitching?"

It was Diana, the background artist, and she was referring to the book that Barry always kept at hand: *The Hamlyn Encyclopedia of Western Films*. A treasure-trove of photographic reference material.

He passed the tatty-edged volume to Diana. She flipped through. "Which one has the weird rocks that look like faces? Is it *Quincey Morris and the Ravagers*?"

"No, *Quincey Morris and the Vulture's Shadow*," said Barry, relishing how his expertise had found a purpose.

"Oh, yeah! I bet this thing's got every Quincey Morris film." Diana departed.

Not quite every film, thought Barry as he did a warm-up sketch of Quincey among the cacti and cattle-skulls. Nowhere did that book mention the film he found most memorable: *Quincey Morris and the Devil-Bat.*

Every Western hero had a selling point. Jesse James had his Robin Hood gimmick; Buffalo Bill was a showman; Billy the Kid was, lo and behold, just a kid. And Quincey Morris? He was *weird.* In his last year alive, he'd headed to the single least glamorous place a cowboy could visit: London. During his stay, newspapers brimmed with reports of bizarre deaths and strange apparitions. Then he and a few mates went on holiday in Transylvania, of all places, where he died on a snowy mountain. The official verdict was murder by robbers, but really, who knew what horrors lurked in the Carpathians?

Such weirdness had followed Quincey his whole life. Some stories about his strange exploits might have been tall tales he'd spun to amuse the ladies, and others made up long after his death, but Barry always reasoned that a few must be true. Law of averages and all.

He remembered a childhood afternoon spent with cowboy hat and cap-gun. A passing neighbour had paused to sneer.

"When I were a lad, I pretended to be in Nelson's navy. So who do you think you are? One of those overpaid Americans, like John Wayne?"

"I'm Quincey Morris," Barry had replied in the best Texan drawl his preadolescent vocal cords could muster.

"Never heard of him."

"I kill scary monsters!" Then, a memorable line from *Quincey Morris and the Thirteen Coyotes* entered his mind. "I've been to the South American pampas. My horse got attacked by one of those big bats that they call vampires."

"What, are you soft? Vampire bats are tiny. They're smaller than the bats you get 'round here."

Even after the neighbour's departure, Barry couldn't let the matter rest. He'd approached Oscar, his most learned school-friend, to defend the honour of their shared hero.

"Well," said Oscar, poring over a school encyclopedia, "apparently in the olden days, people thought *all* South American bats were vampires. And they have awfully big bats there. Look." A grainy black-and-white photograph showed a man alongside a flying fox, which was indeed a very big bat.

"I bet one of those attacked Quincey's horse," said Barry.

"I dunno," said Oscar. "If these big bats aren't really vampires, would they attack horses?"

Neither could answer this quandary.

Not long after that incident, Barry had seen *Quincey Morris and the Devil-Bat*. Nobody he met afterwards, not even the most ardent devotee of Saturday-morning pictures, recalled *Quincey Morris and the Devil-Bat*. But Barry remembered it.

The plot followed a similar pattern to so many other Quincey Morris pictures. Quincey would always ride into what seemed a ghost town, only to find that it wasn't abandoned: the locals were hiding indoors, cowering from the latest spooky menace. The townspeople would do comic relief business while Quincey would be straight-faced and heroic. This time, though, there were oddities. The film was mostly silent, without the typical corny horror music. In one scene Quincey entered a house to find its occupants dead, their limp bodies sprawled over the furniture. Barry still remembered what a damn good job the star did of making it look like he'd stumbled across actual, honest-to-God corpses.

Then came the climax. Barry had expected the monster to be unmasked as a fraud, like the spooks in *Quincey Morris and the Bandits of Ghost Gulch*. But it wasn't. Even all these years later, he could've sworn it was a *real* Devil-Bat on that dark screen.

This childhood reverie consumed him as he sat at his desk, finishing his warm-up picture. He couldn't resist adding one last detail to the scene: a full moon with a large bat silhouetted.

"Here's your book, Mr. Kitching."

Diana handed it to Barry as he walked past, and he mumbled a thank-you. She'd been holding it like an artist's palette while drawing psychedelic designs on the studio blackboard. Nearby, Lew and Dennis had been listening to Rhiannon's anecdotes about a friend expecting a baby or somesuch.

"Do you have any kids?" Rhiannon asked Barry.

He shook his head. "Never met the right girl. Well, no, I *did* meet the right girl, but then…"

He trailed off, not wanting to disrupt the mood. The studio was in good cheer: new episodes had been approved, and the little company had been given new marching orders from its Hollywood higher-ups. This meant more wage-slips and, for the youngsters, more drinks.

"Comin' down the pub with us, Mr. Kitching?" asked Dennis.

"Sorry," said Barry. "I need to draw the new people."

The new episodes brought with them new characters. New for the cartoon, anyway. Barry recognised them as having co-starred alongside George Huston and Randolph Scott and Quincey's other celluloid incarnations.

There was Artie, to start with. Some Western heroes had a faithful Indian, others a cute kid or two tagging along. Quincey Morris was unique in having an English aristocrat as his sidekick. Barry had seen photos of the real Arthur Holmwood, a tall, curly-haired man. In the films, though, the most famous actor to play the role was short, dumpy Nigel Bruce, who lent himself to cartoons. Too bad about the dialogue.

QUINCEY

These Pacific Northwest woodlands sure are mighty pretty, don't you say, Artie?

ARTIE

I'd be dashed if I could deny it, Quincey, old chum! A bloke could fair think himself in heaven here.

Another addition was Lucy Westenra. She'd featured in *Tears of Quincey Morris*, a picture that Barry had never warmed to as a boy: not enough horses or gunplay. The character was based on a fling Quincey had in London. In reality, she rejected his proposal, then she sickened and died. Somehow, Hollywood had turned Lucy from an English rose to a Southern belle.

QUINCEY

Lucy, it's the thought of you that keeps me fearless.

LUCY

Shucks, Quincey! Ah shoulda known you'd be comin' to rescue me from this gosh-darned cave!

Barry guessed that she'd been added to the cartoon to keep women's libbers happy. Fat chance! Those were the people spreading wild allegations of Quincey being a literal ladykiller. Well, the facts seemed a little whiffy, granted: first Lucy spurned Quincey for Artie, then she died under mysterious circumstances, and then Quincey fled the country. But come off it, the man wasn't around to defend himself.

Barry finished doodling Lucy and Artie. The former showed rather more cleavage than the Stateside networks approved, he suspected, but *c'est la vie*. As for Artie, Barry had bowed to convention by drawing the dumpy, jolly interpretation. But he'd been tempted to draw a tall, curly-haired man, like the actor who'd played Artie in *Quincey Morris and the Devil-Bat*. (Who was that, anyway? He couldn't recall. Come to think of it, Quincey hadn't been played by any of the familiar cowboy stars, either).

His next job was drawing the baddies, which afforded greater freedom. The higher-ups paid little attention to a monster designed to be used in one episode and forgotten. Except, Barry liked to think, in the minds of those tykes at home.

He skimmed through the list of names. The Tommyknockers. Hungry Zoe's Ghost. The Phantom Rider on the Hopi Trail. And then something right at the end.

Barry looked again to make sure he hadn't misread. His eyes hadn't deceived him.

There would be an episode featuring the Devil-Bat.

Barry could still recall those boyhood nights spent making effort after effort to recreate what he'd seen in *Quincey Morris and the Devil-Bat*. Cowboy exploits would fade from his school sketchbooks, replaced with fond caricatures of his classmate Oscar and elegant pencil-sketches of an attractive girl, Penny. Over time, Oscar's likenesses grew less fond, culminating in a drawing of a dastardly Oscar snatching Penny away, and both figures eventually disappeared from his drawings, as had the cowboys. Yet the Devil-Bat remained, lurking in sketchbook corners.

Those sketchbooks were now boxed up in his flat, under the desk at which he presently sat, his thoughts far from his schooldays. The only light was a nearby lamp, the darkness around his orange bulb-bubble putting him in the right frame of mind. Those kids could keep their mushrooms or whatever they mucked around with these days: Barry had all he needed right here. Pen in hand like a planchette, he closed his eyes and spilt his memories across the paper.

He gazed at what he'd drawn. No, that wasn't right. It looked like something out of those rubbishy horror comics that got banned when he was a lad. He switched pencils and redrafted the picture in a looser, more ethereal line. Finally, he added some dabs of red ink to simulate the glowing eyes that he remembered so well from the old film. The drawing was finished: Quincey brandished his six-shooter at the Devil-Bat, poised to slay the beast.

And that's precisely what made it wrong. In the film, Quincey *didn't* kill the Devil-Bat. He fought it off long enough to escape, but it remained alive at the end, still haunting the ghost town. This detail set the picture apart from every other horror film Barry had seen. While other monsters returned from the dead, sometimes with a Bride or Daughter or Son in tow, the Devil-Bat needed no such crude resurrection. It was immortal.

Barry tossed the drawing onto a stack of forgotten creations and prepared for bed. He tucked himself in and nodded off, black bats clustering in his mind.

When Barry got to the studio the next morning, Rhiannon approached him with a broad smile that turned her eyes into two creases of eyeliner.

"Hey, Mr. Kitching, we've already finished a bunch of character drawings. Saved you the trouble!"

"Oh, er, thanks."

She handed him a bundle of papers and he shuffled through. A ghostly cattle-rustler, a skeleton bandito, a werewolf with a feathered headdress: all competently drawn, he had to admit.

"Wait 'til you see the Devil-Bat," said Rhiannon.

He froze mid-shuffle.

"Yeah," said Lew, who'd sidled up to them. "She's fab."

She? The Devil-Bat was a lady now? Whose idea was that? Probably Diana, the women's libber of the group. Barry pictured a cartoon bat with fluttery eyelashes and a pink ribbon. He looked through the remaining papers. A hydra-headed rattlesnake. A cactus monster. And last of all, her.

The Devil-Bat.

The drawing dislodged a long-dormant childhood memory. Oscar had told him how sailors used to mistake manatees for mermaids. Barry hadn't seen a picture of a manatee himself, but he understood it was sort of like a dolphin. He'd tried to visualise a dolphin that could plausibly be mistaken for a woman, and his mind had conjured up strange, pseudo-Darwinian hybrids, at once animalistic and alluring. The drawing in front of him was similar; only, instead of a dolphin-lady, it showed a bat-lady. Curves to taunt. Eyes to enrapture. Limbs to embrace. Even a mouth to kiss. And yet unmistakably a creature that'd be at home hanging in a belfry. This wasn't just a cartoon, this was *real,* as though drawn by an eyewitness. Damn-and-blast it all, those kids had pulled it off.

Barry swallowed before speaking.

"This is bloody good."

Rhiannon and the others all grinned.

Break-time came at the studio, and the young animators amused themselves by drawing and erasing doodles on the blackboard. When Barry passed it on his way to make the coffee, he saw a large sketch of a bat, upside-down with outstretched wings. Not the Devil-Bat, just a crude outline of a regular bat with an oddly human grimace. He did a double-take when he noticed that the artist had drawn a nail through each wing, as though it'd been crucified.

"Rather sacrilegious, isn't it?" he asked.

"Pliny said that nailing a bat head-down outside your window will ward off curses," said Dennis, pointing towards a nearby window.

"But this one's inside, not outside," said Barry.

"S'pose it'll prevent curses from *leaving* the building."

"Well, it's a bit sick if you ask me." Barry took the chalk-duster and rubbed out the picture. Disappointed murmurs surrounded him. Then, a grin creasing his face, he drew a new picture: it was the cartoon Lucy as a reclining nude. The boys cheered as he added a chunky dot for each nipple.

Barry turned to see Diana approaching, and he braced himself for a feminist lecture on the objectification of women. He wasn't prepared for what she actually said.

"Hey, Mr. Kitching, we thought we'd invite you to our place for drinks and a toast."

He stared. "A toast? To what?"

"The success of our cartoon. A new series. Maybe better animation."

Before Barry could think of a polite refusal, Lew butted in.

"And we could watch some films on Dennis' projector."

Curiosity got the better of Barry. "What sort of films?"

"Quincey Morris films, of course," said Lew. "We've bagged Super 8 copies from overseas. Not full films, y'know, just highlights, but worth a watch. There's *Tears of Quincey Morris, Quincey Morris and the Thirteenth Coyote, Quincey Morris and the Devil-Bat*…"

Barry interrupted. "The Devil-Bat?"

"Yeah," said Rhiannon, grinning. "We've drawn the Devil-Bat and now she turns up at home!"

For once, Barry didn't have to force himself to grin back. "Alright, I'll come along."

Aside from the problem of a flickering light, the day's remainder was uneventful until its very end.

As he tried to finish off his drawings, Barry heard talking. Evidently, not all of the youngsters had gone home yet. The voices were too quiet for him to make out what they were saying, or even whether it was a boy or a girl speaking. Then he realised it was both. A male and female voice, perhaps more than one of each, were repeating the same thing over and over again in unison. Were they singing? No, not exactly: it sounded more like a poetry recitation. Maybe beat was coming back into vogue.

He tried to concentrate on drawing, but his distracted mind was intent on deciphering their chant:

"Up you fly, bawkie-bird, down you go, bawkie-bird, the hour is here, bawkie-bird, the power shall flow, bawkie-bird…"

Those same words, over and over again.

He threw down his pencil, pushed back his chair, and stormed through the studio. The lights flickering around him, he glanced from desk to empty desk, trying to find those insufferable kids and tell them to shut up and let him work.

By the time he'd walked the length and breadth of the deserted studio, the voices had stopped, leaving him alone in the silence.

Tower Hamlets, Whitechapel, Parfett Street. Of course it was Parfett Street, that prison compound of crumbling flats. If the young animators were paying rent rather than squatting, they were likely the only ones. Barry couldn't object. He'd been a Bohemian in his student days, frequenting jazz clubs and being accosted by teddy boys. His still-younger self would've found the place ideal for his cowboy-hatted fantasies: a veritable ghost town.

He strode past brick walls with windows the colour and opacity of lichen-stained tombstones. As he neared the flat to which he'd been invited, he saw the graffiti evolving from offers of sex, to advertisements for drugs, to such enigmatic phrases as "PAN IS NOT DEAD" and "THE CHILD SHALL BE BORN". When he knocked, the door opened to reveal Diana standing Sybil-like in a dark-shadowed stairwell.

"Hello, Mr. Kitching."

She led him into an upstairs flat. The white walls surrounding Barry were daubed with abstract swirls, song-lyrics and dark-haired women in various states of undress. A Super 8 projector sat atop a cabinet; at the opposite end hung a makeshift screen, its white paper so cheap and flimsy that the semi-naked ladies were just about visible behind it.

Lew, Rhiannon, and the other young animators whose names Barry could never remember were present. Even clean-cut Dennis was there, looking an even bigger misfit than usual.

Barry tip-toed through scattered pamphlets and paraphernalia to the sofa where Dennis sat. He picked up a magazine to make space and inspected the cover as he settled down. It showed a painting of a shapely girl, evidently the model for the female figures daubed across the walls. She was standing in front of a Gothic crypt wearing an outfit skimpy enough to make a *Fiesta* cover-model blush, and it took Barry some time to notice the fangs poking from her ruby-red lips. The magazine was titled *Blooferella*.

"What the hell's this?"

"New comic from America," said Dennis. "It's about the Bloofer Lady. You know her?"

"Can't say I do."

"She's one of the apparitions that turned up in London just before Quincey Morris ran off. There's a tradition saying she was Lucy Westenra's ghost or something, but apparently, Artie

Holmwood didn't like that and tried to stop people talking. There's an article in the comic."

Barry flipped through. Sure enough, the picture-stories in which a barely-dressed Blooferella contorted herself around graveyards were broken up by text articles. "Didn't think this'd be an educational paper."

"Oh, that's a new thing in America," said Dennis. "If it's got enough articles alongside the pictures, that makes it a magazine, not a comic. So they can get away with showing stuff you can't put in comics."

Barry took another look at the cover. "Yeah, she's not the sort of girl you'd see in *Bunty*."

Rhiannon stepped into the middle of the room. She held three small boxes that could only have been the Super 8 reels.

"Okay, which one?" She held up two of the boxes: *Tears of Quincey Morris* and *Quincey Morris and the Thirteen Coyotes*. Rather than poster-art, the covers showed crude likenesses of the actors in what looked like wax pastels. "The romance scene? The gunfight scene?"

The group began chanting like football supporters: "Devil-Bat! Devil-Bat!"

"Alright," said Rhiannon, "*Quincey Morris and the Devil-Bat*!" She waved the third box. Barry squinted, but couldn't make out the illustration. Silence fell as she loaded the reel into the projector.

Images flickered on the screen. Quincey Morris, on horseback, rode up to a forbidding cavern. He dismounted and went inside. He explored the darkness, gun in hand. Then the Devil-Bat appeared.

Barry wondered what had happened to the red eyes he remembered. This Devil-Bat had no colour at all. Of course not: the film was black and white, like every other Quincey Morris picture. Had his memory been playing tricks?

There were other differences. The sequence he'd been replaying mentally since childhood featured a monster whose movements were uncanny in their smoothness. Yet this one had a distinct judder, like the stop-motion dinosaurs made by that Ray

Harryhausen chap. The technique was superior, granted, and whoever created this Devil-Bat could've given Mr. Harryhausen a run for his money. But Barry was left with no doubt that the beast was, in reality, rotting on some modelmaker's shelf.

Quincey shot the Devil-Bat and it vanished in a puff of smoke. The youngsters cheered, but Barry stared bewildered as the truncated film concluded, having run roughshod over his fond memories. *You can't go back*, he thought to himself.

"Wasn't that the one you're always telling us about, Mr. Kitching?" asked Diana.

"It's not quite how I remembered it," said Barry. "Except the actor. It's good they found a man who looked like the real Quincey Morris."

"Well," said Diana. "Some of the people who worked on the film actually knew Quincey when he was alive."

Barry recalled how *The Hamlyn Encyclopedia of Western Films* mentioned Jesse James having a son in Hollywood who helped to launder his late father's reputation, and Wyatt Earp survived long enough to do a similar job himself. But it said nothing about Quincey having such connections.

"How do you know that?" he asked.

With the cheekiest of grins, Diana held up a book. *Hollywood Babylon*, by someone called Kenneth Anger. The cover showed a glamorous woman (was it Jayne Mansfield?) bending forwards, her neckline plunging so far as to reveal her nipples.

"Got lots of stories like that," she said.

Jayne Mansfield. Blooferella. Babylon. Barry was getting too old for all this, and the longer he stayed, the more he felt like either a dirty old man or a schoolmaster who'd wandered into the wrong cafeteria. He stood up, made an excuse about his back complaining, and headed to the gloomy stairwell leading outside.

Barry was back at the studio, spending the end of his shift on a scene of Quincey riding horseback. All was silent, without any girlish giggling or snide comments about flickering lights. He was alone.

Then came a sound:

Ak-ak-ak-ak-ak.

What was that? Definitely not one of his colleagues. Everyone else must've left early, although he couldn't remember seeing them go. Come to think of it, he couldn't remember arriving, either. Just goes to show what a boring, forgettable job he had.

Ak-ak-ak-ak-ak.

Wherever it came from, the noise was distracting him from drawing. He climbed out his chair and set off in the direction of the chattering. The lights were still stuck in their erratic flicker and the room was spending more and more time in darkness. He walked past the blackboard, glimpsing curious Latin phrases.

Ak-ak-ak-ak-ak.

The dance of shadows gave the impression that the studio was breaking into fragments and fractals, with new nooks and crannies growing upon the sprawling layout. In the middle of the black-and-white chaos was a single dark area that stayed constant. He didn't recognise it, but then, he could recognise little in the strobing light. The sound was coming from that pitch-black space.

Ak-ak-ak-ak-ak.

Barry entered the darkness. Which corridor was he in now? The emergency exit? The main entrance? Somewhere he'd never noticed before? He had no idea, yet he pressed on.

Then the light went on with an electric hum. Barry tried to work out exactly what was revealed before him, partly obscured by two vast sheets of leather. Blinking from above to below, he saw first the talons of some huge animal, and beneath them, two limbs of livid skin. Then came a mass of ink-black hair, followed by more white skin flowing into curved shapes. At the bottom was another mass of black hair, but before that was a pair of blood-red eyes. Eyes that sat in an inverted face.

It was a woman, a woman unclothed except for her enormous bat-wings, hanging upside-down from the light fixture by her clawed feet.

White, muscular arms reached out from beneath her wings and grasped Barry by his shoulders.

Ak-ak-ak-ak-ak.

She pulled him towards her body. Her rough grasp dug into his sides as she spun him around, manhandling him until he was upside-down like her. His eyes went from her breasts, which dangled over her collarbones, to her beautiful face. The visage of every woman he'd desired. He wanted her. She pulled him in for a kiss. He closed his eyes and accepted her lips. He reached down – no, upwards – to his flies and unzipped.

That all happened years ago. The events lingered in his memory, but only in the same way that particularly vivid nightmares or wet dreams lingered. A world away from the pub in which Barry sat with his beer.

"Well, if it isn't old Barry Kitching!"

He looked up. There was Oscar, arm in arm with Penny. Time had given them lines and jowls but they were recognisable.

"Oh, er, hello, you two."

"Goodness," said Oscar, as he and Penny sat at Barry's table. "It's been years, hasn't it? Are you still doing those cartoons for American telly?"

Barry shook his head. "That ended back in '74. Now the money's in music videos, at least 'til we're replaced with computers. I've been drawing one of those new bands where you can't tell who's a bloke and who's a bird."

"Funny we should bump into you, Barry," said Penny. "Oscar mentioned you just the other day. Didn't you, Oscar?"

Oscar reached into his bag (the sort the yuppies were all prancing around with) and pulled out a magazine: *The Fortean Times*. "Yes, that's right. There's something here that reminded me of you."

He spread the magazine on the table. Barry peered at the article, which was about some evangelical writer in the US who'd written a book called *Tribulations in the Toy Store*. Apparently, the man thought cartoons, along with the plastic toys that most cartoons nowadays were based on, were made by devil-worshippers. A quotation stood out: "Even the most seemingly innocent Saturday-morning cartoon may promote occult philosophy worthy of the coming Antichrist."

The article was illustrated with various new cartoons. Transforming Japanese robots, loincloth-clad barbarians with axes. Then Oscar's finger jabbed a picture of a cartoon cowboy in a nighttime scene.

"We thought he looked a little like you."

Barry stared at the image. He had to agree: that cowboy was almost identical to the self-portraits he'd drawn as a West-obsessed youngster. Uncannily so, in fact. Then he suppressed a gasp. What he'd taken to be dark, abstract shapes surrounding the central character were actually a second figure.

It was the Devil-Bat, looming over the youthful cowboy. But not in a menacing way: more like the manner of a mother protecting a child, preparing to send Barry's boyish lookalike out into the harsh world.

He swallowed. "What cartoon *is* that, even?"

"Oh, hadn't you heard?" said Oscar. "It's called *Quincey Morris Junior.*"

"That's right," added Penny. "Our kids worship it."

Doris V. Sutherland is a UK-based author who has already done her bit to expand upon Bram Stoker's fiction with *Midnight Widows,* a creator-owned comic about the further exploits of Dracula's three brides. Her other fiction includes licensed tie-ins for the television series *Doctor Who, Survivors,* and *The Omega Factor.* Her non-fiction writing has been published by Liverpool University Press, Obverse Books, Amazing Stories, 2000AD.com, Belladonna Magazine and the multi-Eisner Award-winning Women Write About Comics, where she serves as Books Editor.

The Subsequent Deaths of
Quincey Morris
By S.L. Edwards

Quincey Morris puts his knife through the monster's heart.

The thing beneath him is larger than him. Stronger than him, taller by a whole two heads and wider than the whole world. But Quincey's knife still goes in. Through sinew like red rock and ribs like iron, it goes in.

The thing howls, not unlike a wolf and not unlike a man.

Quincey does not want to look at his monster, to see if it becomes anything else. He's seen enough monsters who look like men. Like women. It's easier, now, to imagine that there's nothing beneath the snarls and the fangs besides animal hate.

There are plenty of stones in the labyrinth, always scattering at his feet and making so much noise that he never knows quiet for long. The one in his hand is only slightly smaller than his fist, but it is hard, and it is heavy.

Quincey strikes the beast's head furiously. Its screams become louder, more terrified—a creature suddenly realizing that death is real and imminent. But the stone in Quincey's fist comes down a few times, the monster beneath him stops moving. The blood pouring from its chest cools. The red streak where a head once was stops producing any noise at all.

Quincey Morris has a mother. A mother he didn't write to much in England, a mother he never told Lucy about because she never asked.

Lucy.

Quincey Morris has a mother. Someone he loved. Someone waiting on him. Would Mina Harker find her? Would she write to Poppy Morris? Tell her that her son was a brave man? A good man?

Or would there be a new drama, a new monster in need of killing?

Quincey Morris died by a river, and he's been in this labyrinth ever since. It can't be anything other than Hell, which he reckons he might deserve. He'd led a mostly good life, but he'd also been a traveler, to places where the edge of one world meets another. The end of Texas. The Pampas. Places where the intrigues of nations and empires met a people's will to survive.

Not even a traveler could get very far without killing in such places.

Quincey Morris had a mother, who suffered a wicked man. Eugene Morris was a hard man, so consumed by hate that it seeped out of him and the very air smelt sour when he was around. He took that animus out on his Poppy, who was as sweet a woman as God ever made. The moment that Quincey got bigger than his daddy, he beat him bloody. Eugene hobbled off on one leg to die in a ditch and lie with the other animal carcasses.

Poppy Morris blamed two wars, one in Mexico and one there at home, for what her husband was. According to Poppy her Eugene was a gentle man until he rode off, though Quincey had his doubts. But she made her son promise, his doubts be damned.

"The Lord don't suffer killers, Quincey. It don't matter what kind. The Kingdom is far too clean for the bloodied."

But Quincey couldn't help it.

After Eugene was dead, there were other monsters. A bandit, who he caught prowling on their farm when he was fifteen. Quincey tried to scare him off, but the man rushed him with a knife. Quincey got him first, and felt so dirty and hollow after that he couldn't even look at the sky out of fear that God's very hand might come roaring down. He buried the man at the edge of the property, and made sure Poppy never got wind.

But there were others. Other monsters that needed killing so other people could live.

There are claws in his sides. His insides feel like fire as they turn to ripped paper. Quincey Morris collapses beside the monster he's killed, which has managed to kill him too.

Quincey Morris has a mother. And if the Lord has any mercy, she'll never learn he's alone, dying again and again.

E ach time Quincey Morris dies in the labyrinth, he always hears the voice.

Hearing the voice, he sometimes wonders what could have happened had he only been a little faster and a little more careful. Would he have gone back home to Texas, finally? Lucy was gone, and the devil would be dead too. What's a man to do, after he kills the devil, other than go home and live-in peace for the rest of his days?

But the rest of his days are already done, and in their aftermath, the devil taunts Quincey Morris:

"History has lost greater men than you. It will lose greater men still. You're gone. I am gone too. But the difference is that while I will continue on, in high art, low art, you are gone.

"The Professor will be remembered. They'll forget he was fat and old. At times it will seem that his story has consumed yours entirely. And your memory, too."

"Arthur will live on too. They'll make him so handsome. Lucy never has any other suitors. Not in the important versions of the stories. She's forgotten you, good man that you were. Small man that you are.

"And they all will, Quincey. Every last one of them.

"But I'll be here and everywhere."

The Devil shows Quincey another world.

This world is black and white, and Quincey isn't even in it.

His knife doesn't feel solid in his hand. The ground doesn't feel real beneath his feet. *He* doesn't feel real, not in this colorless place.

Quincey watches his story go on without him.

Jonathan Harker arrives at a castle. How could the dumb bastard not have turned and run the moment he saw it? The Count greets him and his face is long and narrow. There's the malice, the evil that Quincey recognizes in him. But this isn't the face he met in England. Not the face that snarled at him when he put his knife through the Devil's heart.

There's Lucy. His Lucy. He would've given her the whole world if he could have.

But in this black-and-white world she can't hear him. He calls out to his Lucy, *this* Lucy. She proceeds through this world playfully, coquettishly, flirting with this version of Dracula until it's the death of her.

The Professor is sharp-faced and sharply dressed. He wields a cross just as comfortably as a stake. They confront Dracula in the graveyard, and...

And *this* isn't how the monster dies.

Quincey isn't solid. His heart is racing but he can't feel his hand on his chest. The knife falls to a floor, but whether it is the labyrinth or these colorless catacombs Quincey cannot be sure. He can't even hear his breathing, and can't take his eyes off of this Mina, this Jonathan.

This dead Dracula.

Something grabs at his wrist.

Something pulls him away.

The colorless world snaps away and Quincey is back in the labyrinth, sick with cold sweat and stomach swirling with bile.

For the first time since he's been dead, Quincey Morris vomits.

"You have to be careful to stay away from those places," a soft voice behind him cautions.

The young woman behind him looks to be all of eighteen years old. An ornate dress from a noble household, shining brown hair around her thin face. Her eyes are tired, but kind and perhaps even patient.

She's the first human being Quincey's laid eyes on in this place, and looking at her seems to knock all the wind out of him.

"Dying is hard, but those places...they are harder, in my honest view."

Quincey Morris cannot forget his manners. He is nothing in the world if not for his manners.

He picks himself up and stands uneasily.

He removes his hat, which he's worn all the way from Argentina to Hell.

"Quincey Morris, ma'am."

"'Mam?'"

"Erm...Miss, then?"

"Ah." And the young woman smiles with some knowing in her kind eyes. "Justine Moritz, at your service, Mr. Morris."

When she curtsies, Quincey nearly can't help but snicker.

"Are you...English then, Mr. Morris?"

"What? No, ma'am! Texan!"

"Texan? I'm afraid I've never heard of such a place."

"It's a state. In America."

Justine Moritz's mouth falls open.

"I have never had the fortune of meeting a colonial before."

"'Colonial?'"

Even in Hell, Quincey finds his irrational pride can get the better of him.

Sensing his offense, Justine Moritz immediately apologizes.

"Please do forgive me, Mr. Morris. I'm afraid much has changed since my death."

And her honest apology comes loaded with another hard truth that digs into him just as deep as any monster's claws.

"So...then that's it. We *really* are dead, aren't we?"

Justine Mortiz's smile is sad. Hers is a smile Quincey's worn before, when he promised Poppy Morris that her boy would take care of her after his daddy was gone. He wore it again in the Pampas, when men he never knew were dying and only wanted a sip of water before they left one world for another. And he wore it last when he clapped Arthur Holmwood's shoulder, having done a thing that even Quincey couldn't.

With her smile meant to comfort, Justine Moritz tells him.

"To be truthful with you, Mister Morris, we are. After all, one does not forget dying so easily, do they?"

And Justine Moritz tells Quincey as sad a story as he's ever heard. Of a little girl taken into a loving home, of devoting herself to a new family who gave her a greater life than she could've ever asked for. Of falling for a boy who became a man in front of her very eyes. In some ways, it's a story that he knows all too well, full of injustice and unrequited love. Consigning herself to the fact that the object of her affection was the greater object of someone else's, Justine Moritz devoted herself to a little soul who she regarded part as a little brother and part as a son.

"William." At his name she pauses the story. Quincey returns the same smile she lent him. "Did you have brothers or sisters, Mr. Morris?"

"I've got a little sister. Left her to her husband, though."

"You're a stronger person than I then. I do not believe that I could have left William even if I had an opportunity to do so. The Frankensteins loved me, and I in turn loved them."

She stops.

"Victor loved Elizabeth. I accepted this. It was my belief that if I could not love him as fully as I wished, then perhaps the Lord had charged me with making sure that no member of the Frankenstein household would ever know even the semblance or seeming of suffering.

"But then…"

She stops again.

And she tells Quincey a story. About a young woman out of love, suffering under the weight of an oppressive terror. About a pale little boy with the dark marks of fingers around his neck, and a woman framed for killing him. About the family she loved suddenly, viciously turning against her. And about the look of the man she considered to be her father, who loved her so much that he made her believe dying would be easier than living ever could be.

"I confessed to William's murder," Justine Moritz explains. "But I did not anticipate any divine punishment for doing so. It was my honest view that confessing, lie though it was, would provide some salve for the souls of Alphonse and Victor."

"Then you think you're in Hell because you lied?"

She shakes her head.

"Mr. Morris, I do not believe this is 'Hell,' or at least not so thorough a hell as the Lord visits upon hardened sinners. No, I believe that we are here together because we share something in common beyond simple heartbreak.

"We've both met monsters. Have we not, Mr. Morris?"

Quincey remembers Him.

Poppy Morris said the Lord suffered no killers. For so long Quincey had been afraid of some inevitable, invisible wrath crashing down from the sky.

Then he met Him.

Quincey Morris tells Justine Moritz about his monster. About Lucy, Jonathan, the Professor and Mina. He tells her about the night on the boat, when the others were plotting to kill the demon once and for all and Quincey heard wings beating outside. He tells her about taking his shot at a monster that began as a bat and quickly became the shadow of a man.

Dracula, swaying in a red mist of His own gore. Dracula's face, floating there in the dark. *Sneering* at him. Because the Devil could've killed Quincey then, could've split him in two. A human body, bones, and spine was under the strength of those hands.

But he wouldn't kill Quincey then.

That would come later.

Quincey Morris tells Justine that he believes Dracula was truly the Devil, or at the very least the loyal servant of that old dragon. Quincey had been so afraid of God that he'd never even bothered to consider the Devil. But then, killing such a creature...surely that'd make for a good enough story for the Lord. Dipping his hands in the blood of monsters would *surely* cover up all the blood of the men he'd killed before.

"But now I'm here," Quincey adds.

They're sitting now, their backs to the labyrinth wall. Justine has listened intently, as if the story is just as frightening even after she'd given up the ghost herself.

For a long while, they're quiet.

Then, Justine finishes her story.

The Frankenstein estate hadn't had anything like a jail, no cage to lock the guilty up. Even condemned to death, even having uttered her confession, Justine didn't run. Sure, she thought about it. The night before her death she could already feel the coarseness of the rope on her neck. But in the farmstalls, with the other animals, she took comfort in the idea of redemption. Of sacrificing herself so that the Frankensteins, who she loved more than she could ever explain, could be happy.

But then the monster came.

Justine tells Quincey what the monster told her. How it too was a 'Frankenstein,' more Victor's child than anything that could ever come from his own flesh and blood. That it was just as much an innocent child as William had been, but that it had been wronged by a creator who would never even consider providing it happiness.

"William's death. My death. All they were meant to be were warnings from this monster. That's all they meant..."

Justine tells Quincey that she spent years looking for William in the labyrinth. She was far from the only one there. There had been a British statesman, rambling about some injustice dealt to him by a lumbering hulk of a murderer. Scores of poor souls screaming about horrors she could neither know nor name.

But she was never with others long. When the beasts in the labyrinth came, it was easier to run than to die.

"When you die"—her voice is sad and far away now—"when you die here you cease to exist for a time. And you watch these worlds, these places where the story of your monster has completely consumed your own. To be most honest, Mister Morris, I prefer this place, where I am only *suffering* to the places where I do not exist at all. At least here I know I am real. I know what happened to me. Here I can remember my Victor, my little

William. But there...where I never exist. Where William never even has his story. Then what I did, who he was, who *I* am. I start to question if I even have a story at all, Mister Morris.

"So I'm resolved to live, as one might 'live' here."

"You mentioned other people," Quincey asks. "Do you know where they go?"

She shakes her head.

"I've wondered if these walls change a body, or if they merely swallow them up. There have been moments where I walk with someone, only to turn around and find them gone entirely. It's why I treasure times such as this."

He smiles at her, and imagines he looks as tired as she does.

"Well, I'd reckon I'm grateful too. But Miss Moritz, if you believe there's a way out, I'd be even more grateful if you told me what it is."

"I'm afraid I've no idea," she smiles back.

"Well." Quincey offers her his hand, "Shall we get to looking for it?"

"Of course," she says as she takes it.

The two are hardly quiet as they walk. Justine tells him about the mountains around her home, the thick forests and the quiet peace she used to enjoy.

"I've looked for a place like that my whole life," Quincey responds.

"You've never known a moment's peace, have you, Mister Morris?"

"That's not true. But they've been just that. *Moments*. Little flickers of quiet in an otherwise loud life.

"That's what my daddy said. 'Live loudly, Quincey. Make it count.' When I was a boy, I thought he was right. Even when he beat me bloody, I thought he was right. That a quiet life was a life wasted. But now...now I think it was just an excuse for how cruel he was. After all, he'd had a soldier's life. What could be louder?"

"My own family...I should say, my own *blood*, disowned me. I believe they believed I stopped loving them because I loved the Frankensteins so."

"Did you?" he asks.

"No, I never did. Though their silence hurt me so, I loved them still. They never wrote me, so I would often imagine what they were doing, making stories for them."

"I didn't write my mama, not as much as I should've," Quincey says sadly. "Or my little sister."

"Tell me about them."

"Wouldn't you rather hear about the monster that killed me? Or the warlord who chased me out of Argentina?"

"Mister Morris, I believe that I've grown much too tired of stories about monsters. I've spent enough time letting monsters define my story."

The comment catches Quincey off guard. In England the only thing that anyone ever wanted to know about was his 'adventures.' How had he escaped the caudillo who issued a bounty on his head? How had he fought off cattle rustlers and bandits? How had he crossed the ocean, and what adventure was he planning next?

Lucy had never asked about his family. No one had. He wonders now if they just assumed he was some strong, silent Texan riding out of his ranch to conquer the whole world. Had they assumed some idyllic life for him, not too different from their own? Had they, like Justine, written their own story for him and subsequently never even considered asking him?

Quincey finds it strange, talking about his family out loud. About Poppy Morris, her beast of a husband Eugene, their dead first son Alexander, who didn't live past the age of twelve, and little Abby Morris. Quincey catches himself, because his little sister is a woman now. Abby's sweet as her mother, but she knows men. Men like her father, who was as good as dead the moment Quincey saw him raise a hand to her, and men like her brother, who'd just as soon ride off to cause new trouble than deal with the problem at hand. Her wits and her wit were sharper than either Quincey or Poppy, and she'd made sure the man she married was a good one.

"It's sad now," Quincey muses. "She was a fire-eater, my Abby. But I only met her husband once, and when I decided that

he seemed a good man, I never bothered to consider much else…
but I damn near stopped once. I damn near went back to Texas."

"Was there a problem?" Justine asks. "Did something happen
to her?"

"Yeah, she named her first boy 'Quincey.'

"I was in Argentina, and it was damn near a miracle that I
got the news. But it was either go back to Texas or continue on to
England. I reckon I got on a boat, but maybe it wasn't the right
one."

"Why's that, Mr. Morris?"

"The way I saw it, I did just like my daddy did. I rode off.
And when he came home, the evil he saw and the evil he did took
root in him. Living quietly weren't any good for him, and he hurt
us for it. And I…I couldn't myself hurt anyone like him-"

But Justine stops beside him.

The labyrinth corridor is long, and Quincey can only barely
see the wall on the other side. But now, against it is another
shape. A tall shadow with long, mangled hair.

Quincey steps forward, thinking that they've stumbled on
another person, but Justine grabs his wrist.

"It's him." Her whisper is breaking in tears.

"The monster? From your story?"

"Yes." Her reply is curt. Her hand feels cold.

The monster from Justine's story walks forward.

Quincey can see him now, a thing like a man made from a
patchwork of corpses. He's no larger than the other monsters
Quincey has met so far, but there's a hate in his eyes and a wrath
in his smile that Quincey's seen before. Yellow skin the color of a
long death, and arms wide enough to tear a man apart.

Justine is gasping beside him. Choking from fear, from sad-
ness, from stress.

"Miss Moritz," he yells.

But she collapses.

"Miss Moritz, we should run!"

He tries to lift her up, but she pushes him away. Her hands come to her hair, and her scream eclipses her monster's slow, lumbering footsteps.

The monster gets closer, and smiles wider. Enjoying all the cruelty it's capable of.

Quincey Morris doesn't want to die.

For all the world, Quincey Morris doesn't want to die.

But his knife is in his hands, and his legs are moving beneath him.

The knife goes in, but the creature only considers him for a moment. An annoyance. A gnat.

A hand covers his whole face. A crushing pain unlike anything he's ever felt.

And a woman screaming his name.

In this world without Quincey, the very *colors* are different.

It is lurid, full of pastel colors and blood that seems bright and sweet. Jonathan Harker is dead, but the Professor doesn't know that.

The Professor goes to a place full of castles. There is a Lucy there, but not his. She is not Arthur's wife, but his little sister. Arthur is married to Mina.

Quincey wants to run from this world. To scream that none of this was how it happened. That they've done something terrible to his Lucy, an injustice to the woman he loved.

But this Lucy dies, just like his, staked in a pool of her own blood.

This Dracula has red eyes and a narrow face.

He's killed in the sunrise, and crumbles to dust when the Professor makes a cross from two candles.

The world without Quincey goes on. And on.

Dracula is thrown into a frozen river. He is stabbed. He is crashed into by roaring bright metal machines that Quincey has never seen before.

But he goes on, just as he said he would.

And Quincey is made to watch.

What good did killing him do? What good did it do, if this is all that happens?

"*Mister Morris!*"

For the first time, someone has said his name in this place.

"*Quincey!*"

Justine's hands are warm. She pulls him with a strength that seems superhuman. The lurid world of bright blood and a never-dying Dracula ends.

Quincey is in the labyrinth. In Justine's arms.

She holds him tightly.

"Quincey," she cries, "it is my honest view...that you have an insufferable eagerness to die for others."

And for the second time, Justine's truth knocks the air from his chest and the thoughts from his head.

He hugs her back, softly.

"Well...to be honest myself, you seem to have the same problem, Miss Moritz."

And with that she giggles, sounding for the first time like a girl her age.

"Well." She stands slowly. "I believe, that is something we could work on together."

She offers her hand, and he takes it, lifting himself up as he looks around.

"He's gone," he both says and asks.

"He is," she affirms.

"What happened?"

"You rode off to fight him, ever the gallant adventurer." For the first time, playful sarcasm weaves its way into this proper household attendant's voice. "And it didn't work.

"I've lost so many, Mr. Morris. Victor. William. I couldn't bear losing another friend. And I decided, facing my monster, and all the horror that could come with it...it would be easier than watching and doing nothing."

"Then what?"

"Then he vanished. Simply gone. I don't know what he expected, but it certainly wasn't me, running forward with my fists clenched, weeping and screaming."

"Heh. You've become a warrior woman, Miss Moritz."

"And you've become a bothersome worry, Mister Morris."

"I'll let you call me a 'bothersome worry,' but I'm done suffering this 'Mr. Morris' nonsense."

He takes his first step forward, but falters. After dying, every part of him hurts. There's an ache in his head and at his sides, while his knees crack and burn under him.

Justine grabs him before he can fall and puts his arm around her shoulder. "Should we wait, Quincey?"

"No. No, if there's a way out, I'm itchin' to find it."

"Then I suppose"—she heaves him forward—"you must tell me of all that has happened since I departed our earth. About 'Argentina' and about 'Texas'."

Quincey leans on Justine for a long time. He tells her about history, about the rise of empires and what little he knows about the politics of Europe. He tells her about the prairies, the plains, and the mountains that he's seen. He tells her about the friends he'd made, and the ones he's left behind. He hasn't told his own story in so long he's almost forgotten it. He finds himself remembering small details, funny little things that seem to have gotten swallowed up when he started fighting other people's fights.

When he feels well, he straightens up. "No one's ever let me talk so long before."

"I truly believe, Quincey, that is shameful. Yours is a wonderful story."

He smiles. "Yours too, Justine."

As they turn a corner, a light creeps in. Far away, fluctuating between white and yellow.

"Have you ever seen a light like that?" he asks Justine.

"No."

"Well then. Shall we see what it is?"

As they walk forward, he can see more clearly. Here, there is moss on the brick walls, grass poking up from cracks on the floor.

There's the smell that comes just after a long rain, and the sound of a breeze shaking branches.

"I don't…"

But Quincey stops her.

Between them and the door, there is a shape. A shadow that Quincey would recognize anywhere.

"Is this…*your* monster, Quincey?"

"Yup."

Quincey finds himself overwhelmed by anger. Anger at the monster that defined his life. Anger at the thing that cost him the lives he could have lived, and the people he could have loved.

The monster between them and the way out stands firm. Proud. Spiteful and cruel until the very end.

Quincey wants to draw his knife, to plunge it into this monster over and over again. He wants to bite down onto its neck, and to tear it apart like a beast. He wants it to suffer, to feel the pain that it caused so many people.

But Quincey is done dying.

Justine takes his hand, and he grips hers tightly.

Slowly they get closer, the shadow looming larger before them. When they pass it, Quincey finds the air so cold, so hostile that he wants to run back into the labyrinth, where he can at least die without feeling this cold.

But he doesn't look back.

Not even to see if the shadow truly wore Eugene Morris' face, or something else.

The light grows brighter before them, and Quincey Morris and Justine Moritz continue their stories.

S. L. Edwards is an enjoyer of dark fiction, dark poetry, and dark beer. He is the author of the short story collections *Whiskey and Other Unusual Ghosts* and *The Death of An Author* and the novel *In the Devil's Cradle*.